Keys To Open Your Heart

GOLGOTH ASSEMBLY OF GOD
P.B.No 152, Kanjirapally
Kottayam Dt, Pin 586 507
Ph : 9447564367

Key Publishing Company   *Port Huron, Michigan*

Pastor Jomon Devasya
Golgotha Assembly of God
P.B No.152, Kanjirappally

Keys To Open Your Heart

A Journaling Guide
For Men And Women

Based On The Radio Program
"Today's Key To Confident Living"

by Bill Hossler

Key Publishing Company   *Port Huron, Michigan*

Key Publishing Company
3240 Pine Grove Avenue, Port Huron, Michigan 48060
810-984-5579   1-888-333-KEYS
FAX: 810-984-5595
E-Mail: keys@compucon-mi.com
Visit our Web Page: www:bwb.net/keys

Editing & Design by Justice Communications, 313 Huron Avenue, Suite 202, Port Huron, Michigan 48060   810-982-3908

Cover Design by John Marion

ISBN: 0-9650491-2-4

Contents

*This book is dedicated to six of God's
greatest blessings to Margaret and me.
Jackie, Jeffrey, Jimmie, and Joshua have
each graced our home for 18 years or
more. What a wonderful time it has
been! More recently, we have had the
privilege to welcome Don Weldy
(Jackie's husband) and Shalon (Comfort)
Hossler (Jeff's wife) into the family.
What more could parents ask of God?
Our thanks to Him for each of these six.*

Acknowledgements

Keys To Open Your Heart would not have been possible without those who have helped to keep Today's Key To Confident Living on the radio. The following people have encouraged and supported me in planning, financial support, time and effort in preparing mailings and looking after many other details.

Special thanks goes to my wife (Margaret) and family who spent many nights helping me prepare "demo" mailings. Larry Boulier has provided invaluable help as an advisor and technical support. Kevin Miller encouraged me to pursue other stations when I was on just one station. Kris Overly has given me encouragement to feel this project is by God's clear direction. Ron and Carol Priest were looking for a volunteer project as a couple and they were just what I needed. They took over all the preparations of the mailings and saw that everything was sent out on time. Jack DiGiuseppe was faithful in providing the mailing labels used for sending out our "demo" tapes. Special thanks also goes to Jan Winningham, my secretary, for her enthusiasm for the project and attention to details.

The Key Publishing Committee has been an impetus to see this project through. Thanks goes to Terry Pettee, Art Cooper, Gloria Justice, Colleen Baron, and Ron Flanigan. Gloria helped significantly with her wonderful skill in graphic arts.

The following people have provided special help to me by providing scripts for me to edit: Margaret Hossler, Zaida Chidester, Colleen Baron, Terry Pettee, Kim Phipps, Art Cooper, Mae Lake, and Barb Collins.

A few words of "thanks" seem rather inadequate for all the help you have been.

Preface

Dear Friend,

My work with people convinced me a long time ago that many individuals long for some kind of motivational and inspirational thought for the day. Many of these people are not necessarily deeply religious, but they still have high values. They desire to have a time during each day when they are challenged to live a better and more noble life. Such was my motivation for starting "Today's Key To Confident Living"—a radio program that is now heard on scores of radio stations across the United States.

As the number of stations increased, so did the requests for more and more of the scripts. It was decided to put 100 of the scripts into book form. However, as our publishing committee discussed the project, it was decided to not just publish a book of scripts. We wanted to make it a book that would help readers get the maximum benefit from what they read. It was determined that journaling added that something extra that helped the mind and heart more clearly solidify what it had read. Thus we have added a page to each script for you to write your thoughts, goals and prayers for that day.

We change over a period of time. Hopefully we are in the process of growing and maturing. Therefore, there is a place on the journaling page for you to record your thoughts the second time you read the book. It will be interesting and encouraging to see how God is helping you to become more and more the type of person He wants you to be.

I trust *Keys To Open Your Heart* will become one means for unlocking the potential God has given you.

Because of Him,

Bill Hossler

Getting Started

Dear Friend,

My husband and I have both made it a practice to start each day by reading words of encouragement and devotion. Usually we turn to the Bible, but other inspirational literature can also be helpful. This book is partly motivated by Bill's long established practice of seeking personal inspiration on a daily basis.

More than just a book to read, *Keys To Open Your Heart* also gives you the opportunity to journal your thoughts, goals, and prayers.

Writing these down solidifies what God is saying to you.

What a great way to record the history of your life! Plus, *Keys* provides space for you to write at two different times by each inspirational passage.

As you go back through your *Keys To Open Your Heart* journal, you will be able to marvel at what good things have happened in your life! Make this a source of personal encouragement and a record of your spiritual growth.

Before you read each message, why not ask your loving heavenly Father to speak to you personally in a very special way?

Joyfully,
Margaret Hossler

Time For Action

During a great thaw on one of the American rivers, there was a man standing on a cake of ice that had not yet broken away and separated from the shore line. In his terror, however, he did not see this—but knelt down and began to pray loudly for God to deliver him. The spectators on the shore yelled to him: "Man, stop praying and run for the shore!"

There are times when it is appropriate and right to quit praying. After Jesus had told blind Bartimaeus to "Go, your faith has healed you," it would have been senseless for him to keep on begging Jesus to heal him. The praying time was over and now it was time for obedience.

We sometimes are like the man who finds himself hanging over the side of a cliff and calls out for help. He hears a voice that says, "Just let go." When he asks who is speaking, he is told it is God. The man thinks for a moment and then asks: "Is there anyone *else* up there?" To keep on praying after we have received God's answer is not only unnecessary, but also evidence of a lack of faith or, worse yet, disobedience.

God may have already given the answer to our prayer. Now it is our turn to act with obedience. ♥

Inside My Open Heart...

My Thoughts & Feelings Today   *Date:*

"There are times
when it is appropriate
and right to quit praying."

My Thoughts & Feelings Today   *Date:*

Many have heard the phrase, "and a little child shall lead them." It is often used in reference to a child encouraging a crusty old cynic to soften his heart or urging a couple on the verge of divorce to give their marriage one more try. You may be one who was greatly influenced by your child or grandchild to seek a more noble way of life.

Keep Awake

Children have a freshness and innocence about them that is marvelous. They see life through eyes that are idealistic and hopeful. All of us at one time or another had a similar view, but life has a way of putting cataracts on our eyes of hope. If we are not careful we lose our respect for others, our confidence for the future and even our enthusiasm for living. We often need a little child to awaken us.

The preacher was well into his sermon when, with amazement, he noticed his own son standing at the edge of the balcony and shooting paper wads at members of the congregation below. As the preacher prepared to scold the boy, the youngster cried out, "You just keep preaching, dad; I'll keep 'em awake!"

Have you noticed any children around you recently who were trying to keep you awake? They don't want you to miss out on what life is all about. Even though you may have a few years on them, children may still be able to lead you into a more meaningful life. ♥

Inside My Open Heart...

My Thoughts & Feelings Today   *Date:*

"...life has a way of putting cataracts on our eyes of hope."

My Thoughts & Feelings Today   *Date:*

Life's Too Short To Argue

A husband was once asked the secret of his successful marriage. He thought for a few moments and then shared that two evenings were set aside each week for dining out. They find a quiet place with soft music, candlelight, and good food. After the meal, a slow walk home is helpful...

A friend was about to interrupt when the husband ended his comments by saying, "My wife goes on Tuesdays and I go on Fridays."

On a more serious note, marital harmony should be a goal for each married couple. God intended marriage to be a safe haven from the struggles and difficulties of life. It was intended to be a model of love and fidelity between a man and woman whom God had joined together. Obviously not all marriages are like that, but it can still be the goal.

Disharmony and disputes often revolve around matters that don't have serious consequences. Forgetting to record a check in the checkbook, not putting clothes in their proper places, being a couch potato after supper, or differences in the discipline of children all seem very important at the time, but are they worth the friction and rancor that frequently occur?

Life seems too short to let senseless arguing rob us of its joy and vitality. Ask yourself how important the issues really are. Can't two intelligent people resolve them? Don't hold on to your rights for pride's sake only! Ask God to help you build the kind of marriage He wants you to have. ♥

Inside My Open Heart...

My Thoughts & Feelings Today   *Date:*

"God intended marriage to be a
safe haven from the struggles
and difficulties of life."

My Thoughts & Feelings Today   *Date:*

Quiet Strength

During my morning walks along Lake Huron, I am often stirred by the sight of huge freighters nestled in the fog that hovers over the water. They stealthily make their way toward the mouth of the St. Clair River, quietly slipping between two countries (Canada and the United States).

Slightly larger than three football fields, a lake freighter will slice through volumes of water with little more than a slight hum from its engines. It journeys quietly and with ease—no matter what heavy cargo it's carrying.

There are individuals in our lives who go about their task quietly and stealthily, without any fanfare—bringing comfort to many. It might be a husband and father who early in the morning slips off to work before the children are awake—making no big deal about the effort it took. Or maybe a housewife and mother who toils from early morning until late at night to provide the things so needed for the family.

The Bible says that the one requirement necessary for a person given such a trust is that they are "faithful." They do not have to be flashy or flamboyant—just faithful. Do you have anyone like that in your life whom you could encourage? They have been loyal, devoted and steadfast, but you have not recently told them of your deep appreciation? Why not do it today before you lose any more opportunities? ♥

Inside My Open Heart...

My Thoughts & Feelings Today   *Date:*

"There are individuals... who go
about their task quietly...
bringing comfort to many."

My Thoughts & Feelings Today   *Date:*

Where's The Soap?

A tourist was visiting a village in **Mexico** where a hot spring and a cold spring were located right next to one another. This natural phenomenon proved to be very helpful to the women who brought their laundry, for they could boil their clothes in the hot spring and then rinse them in the cold spring. The tourist commented that the women must be very thankful for this convenience. "Not really," replied the guide. "They grumble that Mother Nature provides the water, but no soap."

Thankful people wouldn't look at it that way. With a unique ability to discern blessings in almost every situation, they can spot the silver lining in even the darkest clouds of life. It is absolutely amazing to me how sometimes people with the most difficult circumstances can be the most thankful.

The late distinguished clergyman Henry Ward Beecher shared a very interesting parallel showing how thankful people are able to see these blessings.

"If one should give me a dish of sand, and tell me there were particles of iron in it, I might look for them with my clumsy fingers, and be unable to detect them; but let me take a magnet, and sweep through it, and it would draw to itself the most invisible particles. The unthankful heart, like my finger in the sand, discovers no mercies; but let the thankful heart sweep through the day, and as the magnet finds the iron, so it will find some heavenly blessings." ♥

Inside My Open Heart...

My Thoughts & Feelings Today   *Date:*

"...sometimes people with the most difficult circumstances can be the most thankful."

My Thoughts & Feelings Today   *Date:*

Tears Bring Rainbows

Someone once said that "the soul would have no rainbow if the eye had no tear."

Nearly a year ago, a friend of ours lost her beloved husband of nearly 40 years. It was unexpected. It happened in an instant. It was a horrendous shock. She says the pain was overwhelming. Family and friends were a tremendous source of support and comfort, but even that couldn't dull the horrible pain she was experiencing. It was as if a piece of her heart had been torn from her body. She felt incomplete as a person for a time. It seemed she was an aimless, lonely drifter.

Through it all she had a deep faith in the Lord and trusted in the power of prayer to move the hand of God. Her total dependence has been upon Him.

Since that life-changing day, many tears have been shed and many new steps have been taken. Many changes, both large and small, have been made.

She's emerging from her first year of grieving like a butterfly from a cocoon. She is becoming a new person in her own right. The joy of the Lord is a reality and she is looking forward to the future now with hope and optimism. She has painfully discovered that "one" really is a whole number.

The Bible says that "Tears may flow in the night, but joy comes in the morning" (Psalms 30:5). "It's true," she says. "I know from personal experience." ♥

Inside My Open Heart...

My Thoughts & Feelings Today   *Date:*

"Tears may flow in the night,
but joy comes in the morning."
(Psalms 30:5)

My Thoughts & Feelings Today   *Date:*

"Middle C" Is Good News

When Loyd C. Douglas (author of *The Robe*) was a university student, he lived in an apartment above a retired music teacher who was in poor health and unable to go outside. Every morning Douglas would stick his head in the door of the elderly man's room and ask, "Well, what's the good news?" Invariably the old man would pick up his tuning fork and tap it on the side of his wheelchair and say, "That's Middle C! It was Middle C yesterday and it will be Middle C tomorrow."

It doesn't make any difference if the tenor singing in the concert is flat or if the piano in your living room is out of tune, true Middle C is always the same.

We often don't know what is truth. Today, we are warned about things that may be thought good for us tomorrow. G. K. Chesterton says that "The scientific facts, which were supposed to contradict the Faith in the nineteenth century, are nearly all of them regarded as unscientific fictions in the twentieth century."

In a constantly changing world, it is good to have something that remains changeless. The Bible repeatedly reminds us that God is always the same (James 1:17). Generations come and go, but God can be counted on to be the same—yesterday, today and forever. ♥

Inside My Open Heart...

My Thoughts & Feelings Today   *Date:*

"In a constantly changing world,
it is good to have something
that is changeless."

My Thoughts & Feelings Today   *Date:*

Melt Down The Saints

When Oliver Cromwell ruled England, the nation experienced a crisis: they ran out of silver and couldn't mint any coins. Soldiers were dispatched to the Cathedrals to ask if the churches had any silver available. The soldiers discovered that the churches had silver in their statues of the saints. When this was reported back to Cromwell, he replied, "Let's melt down the saints and get them into circulation."

Cromwell obviously referred to melting the silver statues, but his comment is an interesting play on words for the church at large. God never intended for those who believed in Him to be garrisoned away in some spiritual fortress. He didn't want His followers hiding behind the four walls of a building located on some obscure city block. He wanted the saints to circulate.

People who attend church offer much to society. Many of them have filled their lives with the teachings of Jesus and the many great leaders from the Bible. They strive to be people of compassion. Godly values and principles are important to them. Frequently they are involved in a variety of community projects. They have the well being of others at heart.

Whenever the church gets to the place of retreating behind closed doors and focusing primarily on show, it is time once again to melt down the saints and get them into circulation. ♥

Inside My Open Heart...

My Thoughts & Feelings Today   *Date:*

"Let's melt down the saints and get them into circulation."

My Thoughts & Feelings Today   *Date:*

A Mighty Force

ornados are an annual part of living in the Midwest. It is difficult to appreciate the incredible power and destructive potential of tornados until you have seen the damage they can cause. Driving through a devastated area, you gain new respect and appreciation for this mighty force with an indescribable energy to change things.

God's power is something like that. We are awed when we see it at work. First, because He can do more in minutes than we can do in months or even years. Second, because it's often beyond our capacity to comprehend such power.

Unless our faith in God is well developed, we usually think in terms of our own strengths and abilities. We size up what we think we can do in accomplishing some task or project. That criteria is used to decide the project's expected outcome. We fail to take into account what God might want to help us do or accomplish through us.

Faith in God's power can cause us to move to a higher level in human living. We need to look at not only what we can do, but what else would God like us to do. When Moses of the Bible was first called to lead his people out of bondage, he sized up the situation from a purely human standpoint. But, God asked Him to look upward—to look beyond his own abilities. The rest is history. You, too, can look upward and discover unbelievable power. ♥

Inside My Open Heart...

My Thoughts & Feelings Today   *Date:*

"Faith in God's power can cause us to move to a higher level in human living."

My Thoughts & Feelings Today   *Date:*

Tooting Their Horn

Students learning about gravity are usually introduced to Isaac Newton and the falling apple. (It was Newton who discovered the laws of gravity in the early 1600s.)

Newton's works may have never been known had it not been for Edmund Halley. He challenged, encouraged, corrected mathematical errors and even financed the printing of some of Newton's most famous works (even though Newton was the wealthier man). A gifted scientist in his own right, Halley seemed willing to put that aside to promote Newton's findings. He had a thirst for truth regardless of who got the credit. His own name would probably have been lost in obscurity, if he hadn't discovered a comet.

Tremendous accomplishments can be achieved if we don't care who gets the credit. Diseases can be conquered, optimistic business goals can be achieved and national problems can be solved when people focus on finding answers—not receiving recognition.

It takes a person with a generous spirit to promote the success and discoveries of others. John the Baptist was such a person. He encouraged people to start following Jesus, even though it cut into his own popularity.

Our greatest contribution may be to encourage someone with the potential to make a difference. Talent and gifts of another may go undiscovered and wasted unless we are "big" enough to toot *their* horn. ♥

Inside My Open Heart...

My Thoughts & Feelings Today   *Date:*

"Our greatest contribution may be
to encourage someone with the
potential to make a difference."

My Thoughts & Feelings Today   *Date:*

Staying Connected

Herbert Jackson was telling his **seminary class** about a car that was assigned to him during his first term as a missionary. The car had just one problem: it wouldn't start.

At first, he got permission from a nearby school to have some of the students give him a push to get it started. From then on, he either parked on a hill or kept it running. For more than two years he went through this inconvenience simply because his car was not getting enough power from the battery. He was proud of his ingenuity and delighted that he had saved the mission a repair bill.

When a new missionary recruit came to take Jackson's place, Jackson filled him in on the procedures for starting the mission car. However, the new recruit was not sure it should be this hard. He lifted the hood, tightened the wires going to the battery terminals and asked Dr. Jackson to try starting the car. Immediately the engine turned over and started. A loose connection had been the cause of two years of frustration.

The Apostle Paul reminds us that the great power of God is available in abundance when we are connected properly (Ephesians 1:19-20). Scores of Bible promises assure us that God is on the side of those who do right. We will have plenty of starting power in every situation when we are properly connected to Him. ♥

Inside My Open Heart...

My Thoughts & Feelings Today   *Date:*

"We will have... starting power
in every situation when we are
properly connected to Him."

My Thoughts & Feelings Today   *Date:*

Not With Disdain

In his autobiography, Mahatma Gandhi wrote that during his student days he read the Gospels seriously and considered converting to Christianity.

He believed that the teachings of Jesus held the solution for the caste system that was dividing the people of India. One Sunday he attended services at a nearby church and planned to talk to the minister about becoming a Christian. When he entered the sanctuary, however, the usher refused to give him a seat and suggested that he go worship with his own people. Gandhi left the church and never returned. He said, "If Christians have caste differences also, I might as well remain a Hindu."

One has to wonder what might have happened if this charismatic and powerful leader had not been so offended by one man's prejudice. We will never know if he would have been able to lead that great nation out of the bondage of the cast system into one where all people are considered equals. One tragic aspect of this story is that great potential for good and God was stifled, because one man developed an attitude of disdain against a certain type of people.

Jesus made it very clear that He cares about all people—not just those of a certain type. He reached out to the destitute, the unlovely, the culturally unaccepted, and the sinful. When asked why He would associate with such people, He made it clear that this was the very reason He came. ♥

Inside My Open Heart...

My Thoughts & Feelings Today   *Date:*

"If Christians have caste differences also, I might as well remain a Hindu."
(Mahatma Gandhi)

My Thoughts & Feelings Today   *Date:*

The Courage To Volunteer

One day a farmer walked into his barnyard and announced that his family wanted ham and eggs for breakfast. He was looking for volunteers.

The chicken quickly offered to help. When the pig failed to respond, the chicken accused him of being ungrateful and just a little bit "chicken."

The pig declined, stating that "It's easy for you to volunteer. You only have to make a contribution, but for me it means a complete sacrifice."

One of the widows of the Bible made such a sacrifice. She only gave two small coins in the offering, but she gave all she had. Even though there were wealthy people whose contributions amounted to much more, Jesus made it very clear that her offering was the greatest, because it required the greater sacrifice. (Luke 21:1-4).

The contributions each of us make to society may not be equal, but the sacrifice required to make those contributions can be. The Bible says that when individuals are given much, much will be required of them. God expects us to use our abilities and means to serve others. He is looking for full fledged sacrifice, not mere token contributions. ♥

Inside My Open Heart...

My Thoughts & Feelings Today   *Date:*

"God expects us to use our abilities and means to serve others."

My Thoughts & Feelings Today   *Date:*

Keeping Priorities Straight

What is really important to you? What do you value most? Do those things that you most treasure get your prime attention?

In January 1984, Senator Paul Tsonagas of Massachusetts announced that he would retire from the U.S. Senate and not seek reelection. Tsongas was quickly becoming a political star. He was heavily favored to be reelected and there was even talk of a run for the presidency or the vice president's position.

Just a few weeks before Tsongas announced his retirement from the Senate, his doctors informed him that he had a form of lymphatic cancer that could be treated but not cured. This unsettling news did not force Tsongas out of the Senate, but it did force him to face the reality of his own mortality. It made him think about the things he really wanted to do in the years he had left.

He decided that what he wanted most in life, what he would not give up if he could not have everything, was being with his family and watching his children grow up. He would rather do that than shape the nation's laws or get his name in the history books. Shortly after his decision was announced, a friend wrote a note to him to congratulate him on having his priorities straight. He wrote: "Nobody on his death bed ever said, 'I wish I had spent more time on my business.'"

How we spend our time should reflect what we value most. ♥

Inside My Open Heart...

My Thoughts & Feelings Today   *Date:*

"Nobody on his death bed ever said, 'I wish I had spent more time on my business.'"

My Thoughts & Feelings Today   *Date:*

The Heart Of The Matter

The story is told of a salesman who was visiting house-to-house in a neighborhood. As he approached the porch of one house he asked the little boy sitting on the steps if his mother was home. The little boy acknowledged that she was.

The salesman began to ring the doorbell. After several rings and no response, he turned to the boy and said, "I thought you said your mother was home," to which the boy replied, "She is, but this isn't my house."

Sometimes we get the wrong answers because we don't ask the right questions.

I have a friend who excels at asking questions. He even has written a book that primarily lists questions to ask in given situations. In consultation with him over the years, he has been able to help me immensely by asking penetrating questions that get me to the heart of the matter. He is able to shed more light on a problem by his insightful questions, than anyone else I know.

Have you ever stopped long enough to ask yourself questions like: "What do I really want out of life?" or "Am I willing to sacrifice my family for a little more money?" or even "How could I get into the job I really want to do?" Jesus told us to ask the question, "What does a man profit if he gains the whole world but forfeits his soul?" (Matthew 16:26)

It is often in asking the right questions that we discover some liberating answers. ♥

Inside My Open Heart...

My Thoughts & Feelings Today   *Date:*

"Sometimes we get the wrong answers because we don't ask the right questions."

My Thoughts & Feelings Today   *Date:*

Hope For Broken Lives

A group of Scottish fishermen were relaxing at a popular seaside inn following a hard day at sea. One of the men was describing a catch of fish—in particular how big they were.

As he spread his arms out to show the size, a waitress walked by with a pot of tea. The story teller hit the pot of tea and splattered its contents on the newly painted white wall. A large ugly brown stain was now located directly in the middle of the wall. The proprietor expressed his disgust. "The stain will never come out. I will have to repaint the entire wall."

"Maybe not," came the voice of a stranger from the back of the room. "Let me work with the stain and see what I can do."

The man took the box he had with him and went up to the wall. Out of the box he took pencils, brushes and some glass jars of paint. He began to sketch some lines around the stained area and then began to fill it in with his paints. The wall came alive with color and beauty. When he finished his work, the ugly stain on the wall had been beautifully blended into a outdoor picture of a large buck with a magnificent rack of antlers. The stained wall had become a thing of beauty.

God is like the master painter. He wants to take our stained and tarnished lives and make them into masterpieces. We may despair that nothing can be done to repair our broken lives, but that's when we hear the voice from behind us that says, "Let Me try. I can help you." ♥

Inside My Open Heart...

My Thoughts & Feelings Today   Date:

"He wants to take our stained and tarnished lives and make them into masterpieces."

My Thoughts & Feelings Today   Date:

The Sore Finger Test

During the time when Calvin Coolidge was running for President of the United States, there were those who questioned his presidential abilities.

Some felt he was "too quiet and lacked color and political personality." Anne Lindbergh was just six years old at the time and overheard some of these conversations. On one occasion she just couldn't keep quiet. She said, "I like Mr. Coolidge." Then she displayed a finger with a bit of adhesive tape on it. "He was the only one who asked me about my sore finger."

A mark of true greatness is the ability to observe the concerns of others. No doubt we have all been touched by someone who noticed something extremely important to us but insignificant to others. We were impressed. We may have only been a small child at the time, but we can still vividly recall the incident.

As we grow older sometimes we forget that small things can mean so much to a child. Learning to tie our shoe or ride a two-wheel bike are milestones from our distant past, but a young child sees them as very significant. They may be the most important things happening in the world of a child longing to be noticed.

The truly great person takes time to notice, to observe, to comment, and to encourage. In the eyes of a child, presidential qualifications may be no more than, "he was the only one who asked me about my sore finger." ♥

Inside My Open Heart...

My Thoughts & Feelings Today   *Date:*

"A mark of true greatness is the ability to observe the concerns of others."

My Thoughts & Feelings Today   *Date:*

Justice
In The
Courtroom

Mayor LaGuardia, colorful mayor of New York City during the 1930s, filled in for an ill judge one cold winter night.

One of the defendants was a poorly dressed grandmother who was charged with stealing a loaf of bread. She defended herself by stating that her son-in-law had deserted her sick daughter and the grandchildren were starving. The shopkeeper refused to drop the charges.

Mayor Laguardia sentenced the lady to a $10 fine or 10 days in jail. But even as he sentenced the woman he pulled a ten-dollar bill out of his wallet and placed it in his hat. He then fined everyone else in the room 50 cents each for the shame of living in a city where people had to steal bread so their grandchildren could eat. Forty seven dollars and fifty cents in fines were turned over to a speechless grandmother.

We don't have to leave things as we find them. We can make a difference. Leaders ask the questions of "why?" and "why not?" They know that things don't always have to stay the same.

Are there situations near you that you have tolerated, but need to be changed? Is there a fresh way of looking at the problem? Is God calling you to be the catalyst for innovation? Is He asking you to be the one to boldly step forward and challenge a nagging and even nasty condition? With God's help, amazing things can happen. ♥

Inside My Open Heart...

My Thoughts & Feelings Today   Date:

"We don't have to leave things
as we find them. We can
make a difference."

My Thoughts & Feelings Today   Date:

It Got Too Big Too Fast

Two brothers in Bridgeport, Connecticut were fined nearly $900,000 for operating an illegal dump.

It had started innocently enough when there was no place else that would take the rubble from the old houses they were tearing down. It wasn't long before the pile of debris covered two acres and was nearly 35 feet high.

The brothers were ordered by the state to remove the material, but the process had become too costly. The thirty thousand dollars that had been spent so far had hardly made a dent in the pile. Thus the hefty fine by the courts.

"It was never supposed to get this high," one of the brothers commented about the large mound of rubble.

How many times have we heard someone caught up in a bad habit or poor moral judgment say, "I never intended for it to go this far," or "I didn't think it would get so far out of hand"?

Bad habits and moral compromise are somewhat like a soft bed—easy to get into, but hard to get out of. They tend to take people farther and they become more sinister than ever planned. It seldom enters the mind that things could get out of control.

The Bible reminds us that it doesn't take much evil to permeate a segment of society, just like it doesn't take much yeast to work through an entire batch of dough. The best time to stop rubbish dumps from beginning in our lives is before they ever start. ♥

Inside My Open Heart...

My Thoughts & Feelings Today   *Date:*

"Bad habits... are somewhat like a soft bed—easy to get into, but hard to get out of."

My Thoughts & Feelings Today   *Date:*

Beauty Of Strong Winds

On a small river in Italy a lumberman was observed jabbing his sharp hook into a log, separating it from the other logs that were floating downstream. A curious onlooker questioned why some logs were separated from the others when they all looked alike.

The lumberman explained that while all the logs looked alike to the untrained eye, there was a lot of difference in the grade of the wood. Many of the logs were from trees that had grown in the valley where they had always been protected from the harsh storms. But, the separated logs had grown high up in the mountains where they had been buffeted by strong winds. "This toughens the trees and gives them a fine and beautiful grain. We save them for choice work," he explained.

How many times have you wanted to get away from the buffeting and storms of life. If you have children, you may have often commented that you did not want your children to have it as hard as you did. You know storms can cause pain and stress.

Yet it's through winds of adversity that character is developed. The Bible says to "consider it pure joy..., whenever you face trials of many kinds, because you know that your faith develops perseverance," which then leads to maturity (James 1:2-3).

Rather than seeking to avoid all the difficulties of life, ask God to help you grow and develop through them. ♥

Inside My Open Heart...

My Thoughts & Feelings Today   *Date:*

"...it's through winds of adversity that character is developed."

My Thoughts & Feelings Today   *Date:*

Time Is A Circus?

Ben Hecht said, "Time is a circus, always packing up and moving away." In Ecclesiastes we're told that "there is a time for everything and a season for every activity under heaven." But we always seem to be saying "I just don't have enough time" or "My, how time flies."

We live in a fast paced world. Almost every time we pull out of the driveway to leave, we are made aware of the fast paced world that technology has created. Man has harnessed mechanical power in numerous ways in order to free us from heavy labor. It has been a successful endeavor, but in some ways it feels like we are now the ones in the harness.

As the burdens of heavy manual labor have been lifted and greater mobility provided, we seem to have gotten busier and busier. We've replaced muscle power with brain drain, which leaves many people worn out and exhausted.

Periodically we need to bring our lives to a halt, sit down, reevaluate our priorities and make time to just *BE*. We need to enjoy recreation at a less hectic pace and not race through play time at the same frenzied speed that we work.

Taking time to sit quietly in prayer and meditation refreshes both soul and body. Even Jesus took time out to rest and pray. We'd do well to follow His example. It's a wise and healthy way to live. Why not take time today?

♥

Inside My Open Heart...

My Thoughts & Feelings Today   *Date:*

"Taking time to sit quietly in
prayer and meditation refreshes
both soul and body."

My Thoughts & Feelings Today   *Date:*

Letting Go

Helmut Thielicke tells of a little boy who accompanied his parents into a gift boutique. As little boys will often do, he began to touch some of the items on display. His parents came running when the little boy began to cry because he could not get his hand out of an expensive Chinese vase. The parents and proprietor pulled and tugged on the arm and vase to get the two separated, but to no avail.

It was finally decided that the only remaining option was to break the expensive vase. In the midst of the shattered pieces, the little boy stood clutching a penny that he had noticed at the bottom of the vase. Had he simply opened his hand and dropped the penny his hand would have come out easily. For the sake of a single penny, a valuable gift was needlessly destroyed.

Sometimes grown-ups also act this way. This is what happens when we needlessly hold on to a grudge and destroy a friendship. At other times, we want to get our hands on a few extra dollars and won't let go—even though it means breaking up our home. Too often, as we stand in the midst of the ruins, we admit that the item we hung on to was not worth the mess we caused.

We need to pray for God's wisdom so we can understand what is important and seek the things of greatest worth. We need to let go of things that are not very valuable in the long run, so we can keep the things that have lasting significance. ♥

Inside My Open Heart...

My Thoughts & Feelings Today   Date:

"We need to let go... so we can keep the things that have lasting significance."

My Thoughts & Feelings Today   Date:

Warning: Hazard Ahead

Joan was taking her mother for a drive. Whenever Joan would exceed the speed limit her mother would scold her. Unfortunately the mother's advice was ignored and Joan was pulled over and issued a ticket for speeding.

As the two continued on their way, Joan complained that the officer should have let her off with just a warning. "Joan," said the mother, "I gave you the warning. He gave you the ticket."

We often get warnings along the road of life, but do we heed them in time to make a difference? How many husbands have been presented with the evidence of a deteriorating marriage but have either ignored the warnings or somehow thought the problems would just go away. Health problems can also receive the same casual response until the time for effective treatment has passed leaving little hope of cure.

God continually throws up roadblocks in the pathway of life to warn us against doing things that are hazardous to our health, perilous to life in general or dangerous to our spiritual well being.

He gives us family, friends, crisis, His Word, the church and even our critics in order to keep us on the straight and narrow. Wisdom reminds us not to be so self sufficient that we can't learn from others and carefully weigh what God is saying to us through them. ♥

Inside My Open Heart...

My Thoughts & Feelings Today   *Date:*

"We often get warnings along the road of life... "

My Thoughts & Feelings Today   *Date:*

Worth The Wait

Are you in a perplexing situation and don't know which way to turn? You're willing to make the right move—if only you knew what that move should be?

Several years ago, a speedboat racer was flung from his seat and propelled deep into the water—so deep that he lost sight of the surface. By remaining calm and waiting for the buoyancy of his life vest to begin pulling him up, he was able to get his bearings and start swimming to the top.

Sometimes we can be too close to our problem to find a way out. We can't see a solution, much less tell which way is up!

During times like these we need to remain calm and wait for God's gentle tug to begin pulling us in the proper direction. His "life vest" will take us to the surface, if we are patient. But how can we get this direction?

■ Quiet your heart so you can hear God's soft and gentle voice. God's voice can't be heard above the loud and garbled sounds of a troubled spirit.

■ Where possible, seek out trusted friends or advisors. Someone who has demonstrated good wisdom in the management of their own life can be of great benefit. Don't try to go it alone!

■ Seek council from books of wisdom such as the Bible.

The writer of Proverbs assures us that if we trust in the Lord and don't just trust our own abilities, God will show us the right path (Proverbs 3:5-6). ♥

Inside My Open Heart...

> *My Thoughts & Feelings Today*   *Date:*

"We need to quiet our heart so we can hear God's soft and gentle voice."

> *My Thoughts & Feelings Today*   *Date:*

I Don't Do Errands!

A beggar sat at the gate of a rich man's home. The rich man was generous, frequently sharing his wealth with the needy.

One day the rich man wanted to send a message as quickly as possible. Since his servants were all busy, he found the beggar and asked him to make the delivery. The beggar was offended. How could this rich man make such a request? The beggar responded by saying, "I solicit gifts, sir, but I do not run errands."

How many people treat their heavenly Father in this manner? They ask and ask for different things and He graciously gives them their requests and more. Then, when He wants them to do something for Him—such as take a care package to a needy family or carry a message of the love of Jesus to a hurting world—they refuse. They may not say it in these words, but it is the same as saying, "No, Lord; I solicit your blessings, but I do not run errands."

Those who are truly grateful desire to give something in return for their blessings. They want to give back to God and others at least a token of their appreciation. To their dying day, they are crying out, "Thank you, Thank you, Thank you."

What kind of a person are you? Do you say "God, I want something, but don't ask anything in return" or do you have a truly thankful heart and say, "Lord, you have been so good to me, is there something I can do for you?" ♥

Inside My Open Heart...

My Thoughts & Feelings Today   *Date:*

"Those who are truly grateful
desire to give something in
return for their blessings."

My Thoughts & Feelings Today   *Date:*

Stare Into His Face

Do you ever get tired and weary and want to throw up your hands and run from everything? "Everyday," you say?

A British soldier was growing weary of the battlefront and longed to go back home. During the middle of the night he left the trenches and started making his way for the coast. Not sure which way he was going he came to what he thought was a signpost. He climbed the post and lit a match. To his surprise it was not a sign post at all, but rather he found himself staring into the face of Jesus. He had climbed up a crucifix that someone had placed alongside the road.

He remembered that Jesus had not run when the going got difficult. Jesus stayed and completed His purpose in coming to Earth. This was the encouragement the young man needed to return to his unit at the front lines.

There are many things that are not pleasant, but running is not necessarily the answer. At times, duty demands that we stay at our post in spite of the dangers or difficulties. You may be a single parent trying to raise your children, a father and husband with seemingly an unsolvable financial difficulty or any number of other perplexing situations. You may want to literally run away from the situation. Running, however, seldom solves anything.

May I suggest you mentally take some time to look into the face of Jesus. The Bible reminds us that Jesus did not run from suffering and therefore is able to help us in ours (Hebrews 12:14-16). ♥

Inside My Open Heart...

My Thoughts & Feelings Today   Date:

"At times duty demands that we
stay at our post in spite of the
dangers or difficulties."

My Thoughts & Feelings Today   Date:

Don't Drop Me... Please!

Have you ever found yourself able to trust God for an unbelievably great miracle, yet lose faith for the simplest of things?

In May 1995, a 34-year-old construction worker named Randy Reid was welding on top of a nearly completed water tower outside Chicago. Melissa Ramsdell reported that Reid unhooked his safety gear to reach for some pipes when a metal cage slipped and bumped the scaffolding he stood on. The scaffolding tipped, and Reid lost his balance. He fell 110 feet, landing face down on a pile of dirt—just missing rocks and construction debris.

When paramedics arrived, they found Reid conscious, moving, and only complaining of a sore back. As he was being carried on a backboard to the ambulance, he told the paramedics, "Please, don't drop me."

Sometimes we resemble that construction worker. God protects us from harm in a 110-foot fall, but we're still nervous about three-foot heights.

There is a story told by Jesus of a man who was encouraged to believe for a special healing. The man had some faith but also had some doubts. He said to Jesus, "I believe, but I need help with my unbelief." Who hasn't identified with that man? Sometimes faith seems to be able to soar for the biggest projects while at other times the smallest need can throw us into a tail spin of doubt. We need to be reminded that if God has helped us once, He is capable of doing it again.

Randy Reid survived his 110-foot fall with just a bruised lung. ♥

Inside My Open Heart...

My Thoughts & Feelings Today   *Date:*

"We need to be reminded that if God has helped us once, He is capable of doing it again."

My Thoughts & Feelings Today   *Date:*

Must Be God's Mom

A lady was shopping in a busy downtown area when she noticed a small child selling newspapers. It was a wet and cold day and the boy was dressed in thin bare clothes. He had no shoes, so he wrapped plastic bags around his socks to keep his feet dry.

The lady felt so sorry for the boy and could not stand to just walk away from the scene. She persuaded the little boy to go with her to a clothing store where she fitted him with some new clothes and a new pair of shoes and socks. The little boy was so excited that he jumped up and down and then ran out of the store. He hadn't taken time to say thank you to the lady, but she sensed that his nonverbal expression was his way of saying thank you.

The lady came to the same area several weeks later and again saw the boy selling papers. This time he was wearing the warm clothes and shoes she had provided. When the little boy looked up, he recognized her and asked, "Lady, are you God's mother?" She shook her head and replied, "No, but I am one of His children." The little boy thought a moment and then said, "I knew you were related to God somehow."

God has no hands but our hands and He has no feet but our feet. As His children, our joy is to extend the work of His kingdom to a needy world. The help you provide may not be to a hungry child or a homeless person but there are people all around us who need what we can contribute. Wouldn't it be neat to hear them say, "I just knew you were related to God somehow." ♥

Inside My Open Heart...

My Thoughts & Feelings Today   Date:

"God has no hands but our hands and He has no feet but our feet."

My Thoughts & Feelings Today   Date:

Finishing Well

The Olympic Marathon run in Mexico City in 1968 was just about over. Only a few thousand people were left in the stands. The winner of the event, Mamo Wolde of Ethiopia, had crossed the finish line over an hour earlier.

Just as the remaining spectators were about to leave, a lone figure was escorted into the stadium. This person was the last of the contestants. He was limping badly from an ugly flesh wound on his knee which he suffered in a fall. Pain filled every halting step he made. As John Stephen Akhwari of Tanzania entered the stadium for the final 400 meters, the remaining spectators applauded him as though he had won the race.

After crossing the finish line, Akhwari walked slowly and somewhat dejectedly toward the dressing room. His Olympic dream had come to a nightmarish end. Someone asked him why he didn't quit after his fall, when all hope of a medal was lost. His response was both encouraging and insightful. He said, "My country did not send me 7,000 miles to start the race. They sent me 7,000 miles to finish it."

Life demands similar courage and fortitude. The reasons to quit are numerous. People often suggest we take what appears to be the easy way out. However, what appears to be the easiest solution is not always the best. Our greatest fulfillment may be in finishing well. ♥

Inside My Open Heart...

My Thoughts & Feelings Today   *Date:*

"My country did not send me
7,000 miles to start the race.
They sent me... to finish it."

My Thoughts & Feelings Today   *Date:*

Gems In Hiding

Some time ago a man bought a rock for pennies at a garage sale. He took it to an expert and learned that he had bought a gem valued at several million dollars. The value had always been inherent in the rock, but it was the competent authority that recognized the value.

Or there's the painting that hangs on a cottage wall—too dirty and discolored to hang on the wall at home. It is an heirloom that has been there for years. No one wanted to throw it away, so it was passed down from generation to generation. An art expert visits the cottage and begins to examine the picture. He cleans and chips away some of the grit and dirt and finds a patch of subtle color that lies beneath, and exclaims with excitement, "Why this is a Rembrandt!" In a moment, the value has soared to unbelievable amounts because of the word of a competent authority.

At times we may feel as valueless as the uncut gem or the discolored picture. We don't like ourselves and we can't see how anyone else can love us either. But God, the expert of all experts, says we have great significance.

The Apostle John reminds us that we are so valuable to God that He sent His one and only Son to the cross that we might be reclaimed. God looks beneath our surface appearance and declares each of us to be worth more than the whole world (Matthew 16:25). ♥

Inside My Open Heart...

My Thoughts & Feelings Today   *Date:*

"God, the expert of all experts, says we have great significance."

My Thoughts & Feelings Today   *Date:*

In His Hands

Do you ever feel like you're carrying the weight of the world on your shoulders? Do people ever say to you: "Lighten up a little... don't be such a worry wart"?

In the entrance to the RCA building in New York City, there is a large statue of Atlas holding the globe of the world on his shoulders. His muscles are bulging and straining at the weight of the difficult task. The load is so great that he can hardly stand up under it.

Many people are trying to do what cannot be done by Atlas—the heralded strongest man in the world. Their life is one of great stress because they try to carry not only what is happening but also what they think might happen. They literally get stressed out, beaten down, and doubled over by the weight of the emotional load.

On the other hand, what if you were asked to paint a picture depicting the image in the song, "He's got the whole world in His hands"? Does that not conjure up to you a God who towers over Earth's tiny sphere and easily cradles this ball of dirt in the palms of His hands? If God can do that to the entire globe then what is He able to do with us? Are our concerns and problems too large for Him to bear? The Bible says, we are to "cast all our cares on Him for He cares for us!

We can either strain and struggle under the heavy load of problems or we can cast our cares on the One who wants to carry them for us. The choice is ours. ♥

Inside My Open Heart...

My Thoughts & Feelings Today   Date:

"We can cast our cares
on the One who wants
to carry them for us."

My Thoughts & Feelings Today   Date:

Power As Needed

I n East Texas there are generators that produce electrical power for thousands of people throughout the southwest United States.

Lignite coal is pulverized, superheated and blown into huge furnaces where it explodes like gasoline when ignited. The huge furnaces turn three giant turbines housed in concrete and steel casings that are 100 feet long, 10 feet wide and 10 feet across. The turbines whirl at 3,600 revolutions per minute.

A visitor to the plant one day asked an engineer where the electricity was stored. "It is not stored" he replied. "It is produced as it is needed." When a person turns on a light switch in Dallas the meters at the plant detect that more power is needed and more is generated.

The way God supplies our power is similar to that of the generating plant. As we need more power, it is made available to us. There are no huge storage batteries built into us nor a great power grid somewhere in the heavens that has unlimited supplies of God's resources. We receive strength and power as they are needed. The Bible makes it clear that our strength will be equal to our days (Deuteronomy 33:25).

Don't worry about having enough strength to make it through today and for sure don't worry about tomorrow. Ask God to give you what you need right now. Start drawing on the strength that is available and more will be given as needed. ♥

Inside My Open Heart...

My Thoughts & Feelings Today   *Date:*

"Start drawing on the strength that is available and more will be given as needed."

My Thoughts & Feelings Today   *Date:*

Spiritual Heart Surgery

Heart bypass surgery, once dreaded and thought almost impossible, is now frequently performed in big city hospitals and smaller regional centers.

One thing is considered essential. During the process of preparing for heart surgery the doctor asks the patient for permission to do the surgery—and even asks for it in writing. Without this signature the surgeon would only begin in the case of a life-threatening emergency. The doctor doesn't ask the patient to help supervise the surgery, hold the scalpel, or apply the anesthetic. He only asks for authorization. The same thing is necessary when God wants to do spiritual heart surgery on us.

God wants permission. Too often we want to direct and supervise the process. We want Him to do only what we feel comfortable with and nothing more. We try to tell Him how to do His work. The result is that we put on band-aids or superficial cosmetic cover ups that don't cure the problem. We need to give the Great Physician permission to take whatever steps are necessary to fix our heart.

The Psalmist David sought such heart surgery when he said, "Create in me a new, clean heart, O God, filled with clean thoughts and right desires" (*Living Bible*, Psalms 51:10). ♥

Inside My Open Heart...

My Thoughts & Feelings Today   Date:

"We need to give the Great Physician permission to... fix our heart."

My Thoughts & Feelings Today   Date:

Imprisoned By Choice

Do habits and appetites control you or do you control them? Thomas Costain's history, *The Three Edwards*, describes the life of Raynald III, a fourteenth-century duke in what is now Belgium. Raynald was grossly overweight. He was fat. After a violent quarrel, Raynald's younger brother Edward led a successful revolt against him.

Captured but not killed by Edward, Raynald was confined to a room especially built for him in the Nieuwkerk Castle. He was promised his title and property as soon as he was able to leave the room. For most people this would not have been difficult, since the room had several windows and a door of near-normal size, and none were locked or barred. The problem was Raynald's size. To leave the room, Raynald needed to lose weight. But knowing his older brother, Edward sent him a variety of delicious foods. Raynald could not refuse and indulged his appetites rather than take control of his life.

When Duke Edward was accused of cruelty, he had a ready answer: "My brother is not a prisoner. He may leave when he so wills." Raynald stayed in that room for ten years and wasn't released until after Edward died in Battle. By then his health was so ruined he died within a year—a prisoner of his own appetite.

If you feel imprisoned by your appetites and habits, look toward the open door of freedom. With God's help you can take control of your life and become the person He designed you to be. ♥

Inside My Open Heart...

My Thoughts & Feelings Today   *Date:*

"With God's help... take control of your life and become the person He designed you to be."

My Thoughts & Feelings Today   *Date:*

With A Grateful Heart

An Associated Press story told how tourists and residents of North Carolina were spared from the devastation of Hurricane Emily on September 1, 1993. The hurricane touched the tip of the United States at Cape Hatteras and miraculously turned back into the Atlantic Ocean.

The relief was symbolized by a spray-painted plywood sign which read, "Dear Emily, Sorry We Missed You. Thanks for the Waves. Sincerely, Your Locals."

Do you stop and think how many times the hurricanes of life have passed you by? Things could have been so much worse. Your situation had the potential for a devastating storm of conflict, physical pain, marital strife or even loss of life, but you escaped with just some wind and waves of difficulty.

The Psalmist had experienced such kinds of help so he wrote, "Let everyone who is godly pray to you...; surely when the mighty waters rise they will not reach Him, you are my hiding place; you will protect me from trouble and surround me with songs of deliverance" (Psalms 32:6-7).

As we develop the attitude of the grateful heart, we will more quickly spot the hurricanes of life and how the Lord helped them to pass just to the side of us. It is out of such gratitude that people see a countenance and demeanor that is to them peaceful and tranquil. Don't be too surprised if you find people asking you what makes you so happy and contented. Be sure to tell them about some of the hurricanes that just passed you by.

♥

Inside My Open Heart...

My Thoughts & Feelings Today   Date:

"Be sure to tell them about some of the hurricanes that just passed you by."

My Thoughts & Feelings Today   Date:

**Save
The Day**

A quote from *Heart Warmers* says
that "Each day is God's gift to you,
make it blossom and grow into a
thing of beauty." It's a great line to
remember when we get up in the morning—
especially when we get up on the wrong side
of the bed.

Picture this: The alarm goes off and rudely
awakens you from a sound and relaxing sleep.
It's too soon. You're too tired. It seems like
you had just gotten to sleep and it is time to
get up again.

Someone has forgotten to set the timer so
there is no aroma of fresh-brewed coffee to
tease you into wakefulness. Your youngest
child has finished the last of the breakfast
rolls. Your teenage daughter is monopolizing
the bathroom and you're beginning to run a
little bit late.

Instead of wanting your day to blossom,
you'd rather bury it in the sand and walk away
from it. You don't expect anything to bloom
except one colossal headache. You find
yourself wondering where it all went wrong.

You don't need to wait for tomorrow to
salvage the day. It can still blossom into a
thing of beauty. Take a few minutes to relax
and gather your thoughts. Focus on all the
good things in life: a loving spouse, healthy
children and a job that you really do enjoy
most days. Whisper a short prayer thanking
the Lord for all the good things in your life
and then remember what the Bible says, "This
is the day the Lord has made; let us rejoice
and be glad in it" (NIV, Psalms 118:24). ♥

Inside My Open Heart...

My Thoughts & Feelings Today   *Date:*

"You don't expect anything to bloom except one colossal headache."

My Thoughts & Feelings Today   *Date:*

Impressions In The Sand

A father took his six-year-old son fishing out on the lake. The dad wanted this to be one of those great days for bonding and memories.

He made sure he had all the right equipment so there would be no excuse for a bad day. The father and son got out of the car, trekked down across the beach and out to the boat. They fished all morning and then went back to shore at noon. They tied up the boat and trekked back up the beach.

During lunch, the father wanted to find out what had impressed his young son the most about the outing. Was it all the gear we had to work with? Was it the nice boat we used to fish from? Was it the large number of fish we caught? These things were all nice but they were not the things that seemingly impressed the boy who said, **"I liked it best when I tried to walk in your foot prints across the sand."**

Something the father hadn't even noticed became for the son the most meaningful part of the entire outing. Furthermore, it was a son trying to be like his dad that may have been the greatest lesson learned that day.

Our children develop attitudes and patterns of behavior like us when we aren't even aware of it. In fact, our times of greatest teaching may be when we are observed just going about our daily insignificant tasks and not the times we intentionally attempt something meaningful. ♥

Inside My Open Heart...

My Thoughts & Feelings Today   *Date:*

"...children develop attitudes and patterns of behavior like us when we aren't even aware..."

My Thoughts & Feelings Today   *Date:*

When Faith Turns To Fear

Many of you recognize the name Wallenda as the world's greatest family of aerialists and tightrope walkers. Karl Wallenda, the patriarch of this family, had the unique ability to concentrate on the task at hand and perform some incredible feats. Often he would go into a city, have his crew string a high wire between two buildings and then proceed to walk across it. He did this for years. But then one day in San Juan, Puerto Rico, he fell to his death while trying to walk between two high rise buildings without a safety net.

His wife later commented that, shortly before his fall, he had started to talk about falling—something she had never heard him say before. He had also supervised the rigging of the wire—a job previously left entirely to others. It appears he had begun to think more about falling than successfully traversing the wire. His faith had turned to doubt and fear.

Do you remember the Bible story where Peter wanted to walk on the water to Jesus? Peter was getting along fine until he got his eyes off the Lord and started looking at the waves. When he took his eyes off the source of his help and began to look at the potential for failure, he started to sink.

Peter's faith turned to fear and doubt because he concentrated more on failing than success. Faith and success reside in the Source of our help, while fear and failure result from looking at the waves of our lives.

♥

Inside My Open Heart...

My Thoughts & Feelings Today   *Date:*

"...fear and failure result from looking at the waves of our lives."

My Thoughts & Feelings Today   *Date:*

Stepping Stones

One failure doesn't have to mean we're finished. One of the greatest revelations to me when starting in my career was to learn that leaders expected to fail some times. They didn't always succeed. But, neither were they failures just because they had some failures. We don't like to make mistakes but the person who never makes mistakes or has failures is the person who isn't doing anything.

One of my favorite quotes is by President Teddy Roosevelt when he said, "Far better it is to dare mighty things, to win glorious triumphs, even checkered by failure, than to take rank with those poor spirits who neither enjoy much nor suffer because they live in the gray twilight that knows not victory nor defeat."

One ball player set the major league record for strike-outs with 1,316. The same player set a record for five consecutive strike-outs in a World Series game. You'd probably think twice about having that player on your team. That is, until you found out that the holder of both records was the great slugger Babe Ruth. The fact that we don't always succeed doesn't mean our lives can't be successful!

God does not want our failures to finish us. Many stories in the Bible deal with people who failed, but you consistently see God picking them up and helping them go on. Don't let failure get the best of you. Let God help you regroup and go on. Failures can be stepping stones if we allow them to be. ♥

Inside My Open Heart...

My Thoughts & Feelings Today   Date:

"God does not want our failures to finish us."

My Thoughts & Feelings Today   Date:

Avoid Running On Empty

Do you remember seeing the old oil lamps that had one end of the wick immersed in oil and the other raised or lowered by a little round knob? If you collect antiques or enjoy modern day replicas, you may have one in your home.

I have been fascinated by these lamps for some time. It is amazing how long the wicks can burn before needing to be replaced. You would think the fire on the end of the wick would quickly consume it, but it doesn't.

Of course, the secret of its lasting power is the oil in the reservoir. As long as the wick is saturated with the proper oil it will continue to burn with a warm and soothing light. It casts a very pleasing glow around a darkened room. However, once the oil is consumed and the wick dries out, it is quite another story. The wick begins to smoke and be consumed by the fire. The lamp that once gave off a warm and inviting light becomes smokey, offensive and before long useless.

Humans are a lot like these lamps. What we are on the outside is based on what we have on the inside. If we have plenty of God's Spirit, then we are able to be a light of hope, warmth and pleasantness in spite of the darkness around us. But if we try to run on empty, with the fuel of His Spirit having been all drained out or used up, then before long others will begin to notice. We will become irritable, offensive and useless.

Regularly, we need to be refueled so we can be refired. It doesn't take long, but it is vitally important. ♥

Inside My Open Heart...

My Thoughts & Feelings Today   Date:

"...we are able to be a light of
hope, warmth and pleasantness
in spite of the darkness..."

My Thoughts & Feelings Today   Date:

The Lost Violin

One cold wintry afternoon a haggard looking man made his way into a music shop in London. The oblong case he held under his arm gave no indication of the surprising outcome of the story.

Wanting to get some money for food, the man placed his case on the counter and asked the proprietor to purchase its contents. After receiving the equivalent of less than $20, the man hurried out into the frigid night air.

All alone, the shop owner opened the case and put the old violin to his chin and pulled the bow across the strings. The sound of this violin was unusual. Its rich, pure and melodious sound was like few he had ever heard. He peered inside the violin to see if there was any kind of a trademark or insignia that would distinguish this violin from others. To his great surprise, he saw the magic name of Antonio Stradivari and the date of 1704. He immediately knew this was the famed violin that all Europe had been looking for. Eventually, it was sold for several hundreds of thousands of dollars.

The tragic part of this story is that the haggard looking man who sold the violin for a little food money had more than he needed for a long time sitting right under his nose and just didn't recognize it.

Aren't we just like him sometimes? Do we keep thinking about "some other time... some other place... some other person"?

Rather than conclude that we don't have the right resources, why not discover the priceless treasures that are all around us! ♥

Inside My Open Heart...

My Thoughts & Feelings Today   *Date:*

"...why not discover the priceless treasures that are all around us!"

My Thoughts & Feelings Today   *Date:*

Impact Of Little Things

T he sign on the front lawn of a church read: "Mosquitoes remind us that little things can make a big impact." Most of us have experienced the effects of one or more of these "little things"... a popcorn kernel stuck in your tooth, a pebble in your shoe, a pimple on your face, a thank you, a hug, or simply saying, "I'm sorry."

In the Bible, James tells about three other little things that can make a big impact: a bit in a horses mouth, a rudder of a ship, and the tongue. James goes on to say that the tongue is a small part of the body, yet it can corrupt the entire person and set the whole course of his life on fire (James 3). How can this little muscle in the mouth cause so many problems? How can it get so many people in so much trouble? On the one hand, this tongue can be gracious, kind, and encouraging while nearly the next minute it can be used for cursing, ridiculing and downgrading remarks. How can this be?

James reminds us that while we are engaged in training for about everything else, we also need to train our tongue to serve us for good—not evil. We need to learn to bring it under the control of self-discipline. The Psalmist went one step further and asked God to "Set a guard over my mouth... and keep watch over the door of my lips." (Psalms 141:3) That is good advice so that one of the little things doesn't trip us up. ♥

Inside My Open Heart...

My Thoughts & Feelings Today   *Date:*

"How can this little muscle in the mouth cause so many problems?"

My Thoughts & Feelings Today   *Date:*

Details Of Apollo 13

The producers of the movie *Apollo 13* amazingly portrayed thousands of genuine technical details in the story of NASA's great rescue. But, leave it to a few NASA engineers at the Johnson Space Center to point out some of the things that the movie didn't get right.

In the movie, a technician at the Cape wears a Rockwell International logo on his coveralls. The Apollo capsule was built by North American, which did not become Rockwell until after the Apollo program. In the real life version, the engines of the Saturn V were started at T-9 seconds, not zero as portrayed in the movie. The Gantry Arms for the Saturn V were released in unison, not one at a time. The Flight Director was never called "Gene" as in the movie, but by his call sign "Flight," or Mr. Krantz. And at the time of the original launch, Mission Control Center was just labeled "30" and not "Building 30 N" as it is now.

While these keen insights into the movie's errors might help us win a trivia game sometime in the future, always looking for minute flaws in others can be damaging to our own growth and development. When we become enamored with hunting for specks in life's picture, we will be consumed by the imperfections. Jesus said in Luke 6:42, "How can you say to your brother, 'Brother, let me take the speck out of your eye,' when you yourself fail to see the plank in your own eye? ....first take the plank out of your eye, and then you will see clearly to remove the speck from your brother's eye." ♥

Inside My Open Heart...

My Thoughts & Feelings Today   *Date:*

"...always looking for minute flaws in others can be damaging to our own growth..."

My Thoughts & Feelings Today   *Date:*

Are You A Fish?

Bathyspheres or fish—which one are you like? Jay Kesler in *Campus Life* magazine writes that:

"There are two ways of handling pressure. One is illustrated by a bathysphere, the miniature submarine used to explore the ocean in places so deep that the water pressure would crush a conventional submarine like an aluminum can. Bathyspheres compensate with plate steel several inches thick, which keeps the water out but also makes them heavy and hard to maneuver. Inside they're cramped. When these craft descend to the ocean floor, however, they find they're not alone. When their lights are turned on and you look through the tiny, thick plate glass windows, what do you see? Fish! These fish cope with extreme pressure in an entirely different way. They don't build thick skins: they remain supple and free. They compensate for the outside pressure through equal and opposite pressure inside themselves. Christians, likewise, don't have to be hard and thick skinned—as long as they appropriate God's power within to equal the pressure without."

The apostle Paul prayed this way (Ephesians 3:16): "I pray that out of his glorious riches he may strengthen you with power through his Spirit in your inner being..." You see, when all the world is trying to collapse your small frame, Christ wants you to have His strength pushing out from inside you. ♥

Inside My Open Heart...

My Thoughts & Feelings Today   *Date:*

"...Christ wants you to have His strength pushing out from inside you."

My Thoughts & Feelings Today   *Date:*

Don't Fuel The Fire

The fundamental theory of putting out a fire remains unchanged. A major goal in extinguishing a blaze is to remove one of the essential elements needed for fueling the fire.

For example, such a principle is often used in fighting a forest fire. A controlled backfire is started from a cleared line ahead of the advancing flames. When the two fires meet, no timber is left to burn.

The Bible says, "...as wood is to a fire, so is a quarrelsome man for kindling strife" (Proverbs 26:21). Just as adding wood to a fire keeps the fire burning, so adding words and actions of contention keep many quarrels fueled. How many relationships have been scarred and homes destroyed because of the fuel of angry words? But by following a few simple principles we can make considerable improvement. We need to:

1. Listen before we speak. That is why God gave us two ears but only one tongue.

2. Think before we speak. Are the words I am thinking about saying appropriate for the situation? Is this quarrel going to be worth the damage it will cause?

3. Don't always demand our rights. Our rights can sometimes get in the way of the quick resolution of a matter.

4. Try to be rested before responding to quarrelsome situations. Sometimes a hasty letter written in anger before retiring is destroyed after a night's rest.

The Bible tells us to do what we can to live at peace with everyone (Romans 12:18).
♥

Inside My Open Heart...

My Thoughts & Feelings Today   *Date:*

"...adding words and actions of contention keep many quarrels fueled."

My Thoughts & Feelings Today   *Date:*

Anger puts a person at a disadvantage in almost every undertaking in life. When Sinbad and his sailors landed on one of their tropical islands, they were very thirsty. Looking around they saw high up in the trees coconuts which could quench their thirst and satisfy their hunger.

Angry Monkeys

The sailors were not able to reach the coconuts, but high in the branches of the trees were the chattering apes. Sinbad and his men began to throw stones and sticks up at the apes. The enraged monkeys began to seize the coconuts and hurl them down at the men on the ground. That was just what Sinbad and his men wanted. The men never had to leave the ground to gather their food. The angry monkeys did it for them.

Our indulgence in anger plays into the hands of our enemies. The Bible says we are not to let the sun go down while we are still angry (Ephesians 4:26). What good advice! Just think what would happen in our homes and work places, if we resolved all our angry conflicts before nightfall?

But how can we overcome anger? How can we get things settled before night time? A few simple steps may be helpful. 1) Determine to make anger resolution a top priority. 2) Deal quickly with the feelings of anger that well up within you. 3) Frequently use the phrase, "I am sorry." 4) Choose to be a peace maker. Deal quickly with your anger so that it doesn't work to your disadvantage. ♥

Inside My Open Heart...

My Thoughts & Feelings Today   Date:

"Our indulgence in anger
plays into the hands
of our enemies."

My Thoughts & Feelings Today   Date:

Never Growing Old

Some years ago, the discovery of a drug that could bring about a lifespan of up to 200 years was claimed by a research team at Michigan State University.

They believed if experiments proved right, it would make lower body temperatures possible and thus slow the aging process.

Is there a difference between aging and getting old? I think so. How do you look at life? Are you a worrier or chronically pessimistic? Do you dislike new ideas just because they're different? Do you resist change and like the rut you live in? If you answer yes, you're on the fast road to getting old. If you say no, you'll be forever young. You're the type of person who greets each new day with enthusiasm and a joyful spirit. You have an open mind and heart and are alert for new ideas and opportunities.

"Old" is a state of mind. People can be old at twenty and young at eighty. It depends on attitude. You can choose to be an old youngster or a young oldster. Which are you? Are you a victim of "old" disease or are you a treasure chest full of youthful enthusiasm?

Bernard Baruch said that "To me, old age is fifteen years older than I am." Do you concur? With this view of aging, you'll never get "old". You'll mature and improve with age. You may live a great number of years, but old you'll never be. Think about it. ♥

Inside My Open Heart...

My Thoughts & Feelings Today   *Date:*

"You can choose to be an old youngster or a young oldster."

My Thoughts & Feelings Today   *Date:*

Security

Stephen Pile in the book *Cannibals in the Cafeteria,* **tells about a Canadian pacifist** who sold his home and moved to a place he thought would be peaceful—far from the rumblings of war.

After months of studying a world map to find *the* safest retreat, he was sure his new home would be far from guns and war. In March of 1982 he moved to the Falkland Islands—just five days before the Argentinians invaded this quiet island, starting the Falklands War.

We all long for some means of securing our peace and safety. We try to shield ourselves and our children from as many dangers as possible. We try to eat right to ward off certain diseases and emphasize exercise to make our hearts stronger. We keep our children out of certain environments to protect them from evil people. But, we don't always succeed in spite of our efforts.

We can become almost paralyzed with fear over things that might happen. We can lose our sense of joy in living. Paranoid feelings of danger can consume large chunks of our waking hours. But does God want us to live like that? Does He want unwholesome fear to sap our energy and to steal our enthusiasm? Consider the following:

The Psalmist had ample reason to have feelings of fear, but he comforted himself with thoughts of his God. In Psalm 27:1 David wrote, "Though an army besiege me, my heart will not fear." He furthered added, "The LORD is my light and my salvation—whom shall I fear? The LORD is the stronghold of my life—of whom shall I be afraid?" ♥

Inside My Open Heart...

My Thoughts & Feelings Today   *Date:*

"We all long for some means of securing our peace and safety."

My Thoughts & Feelings Today   *Date:*

Going The Second Mile

Right attitudes can breed success. Twenty people may start out in life at approximately the same place, but some will make the grade and others won't. Why? What makes the difference? In many cases it is simply a matter of having the right attitude.

The story is told about a shoe salesman who was sent to Africa to sell shoes. He was not there very long until discouragement got the best of him and he headed back to America. When asked why he came home, he dejectedly replied that "No one wears shoes over there."

Another salesman was sent in the first man's place and he kept calling for more orders of shoes—sales were great. When asked how he did it, he responded that "everybody over here needs shoes."

Positive minded people develop a "we can do it" mentality. Obstacles may block their way now and then, but they have learned how to either remove them or go around them.

Positive minded people are also "second milers." They have a spirit of service and are willing to do far more than required. Jesus coined the "second miler" phrase when He said, "If someone orders you to go one mile, go with him two miles" (Matthew 5:41).

The prospect of your life being successful depends primarily on you. Seeing possibilities through the eyes of faith and being known as a joyful "second miler" will do much to propel you down the road to effective living. ♥

Inside My Open Heart...

My Thoughts & Feelings Today   Date:

"A person with a right and positive attitude sees possibilities."

My Thoughts & Feelings Today   Date:

Rippling Tones

The *Sunshine Magazine* tells about a joint project conducted by a speech research unit at Kenyon College and the United States Navy. The purpose was to discover how the tone quality of the voice affected sailors when they were given orders.

A number of experiments revealed that the way a person was addressed determined to a large extent the kind of response he would make. For example, a soft voice usually elicited a soft response. Conversely, when a person was shouted at, the reply usually came back in the same sharp tones. This was true whether the communication was given face-to-face, over the intercom, or by telephone.

The writer of the Proverbs (15:1) was right when he said, "A gentle answer turns away wrath, but a harsh word stirs up anger." The way we speak to others has much to do with the response we get back. If we are soft spoken, gentle, kind and considerate, then the responses we get back will probably be in a similar manner. But, if we are caustic, sharp, critical and boisterous, we shouldn't be surprised if we get similar treatment.

Sometimes we may not realize how we are speaking to others. We may be having a bad day or are frustrated with another situation but our tension is reflected in our speech. To hear how we sound to others, we may only have to listen how they sound to us. Many times people are only parroting the words we have just spoken to them. ♥

Inside My Open Heart...

My Thoughts & Feelings Today   *Date:*

"The way we speak to others has much to do with the response we get back."

My Thoughts & Feelings Today   *Date:*

Like A Bamboo Tree

Are your children late bloomers? Did they have several years with little growth and then seemingly overnight were looking you eye-to-eye? That's the way it was with our three boys.

I would hear, "Dad, I'm the shortest boy in my class. Am I *ever* going to get bigger?" I would remind them that in Junior High I was referred to as "little Bill" until I hit my growth spurt. My wife and I reassured them that if they ate right, got good rest, exercised and were not affected by some physical problem, nature would take its course and they would get taller. And they did. It's not that they weren't developing during those early years—they just weren't growing upward.

The Chinese bamboo tree shows almost no signs of growth for the first four years. Then during the fifth year it grows ninety feet in sixty days. Is the tree doing anything during the first four years? Certainly those early years affect its later development.

You may be working on a project that seems to be going nowhere. You have tried and tried and tried, but with few visible results. Remember, if you do the right things long enough you will get positive results. You will be rewarded just as surely as our children will grow. Results may come as slowly as with the bamboo tree, but they will come. The Scriptures remind us that we will reap in accordance with whatever we have sown (Galatians 6:7). ♥

Inside My Open Heart...

My Thoughts & Feelings Today   *Date:*

> "...if you do the right things
> long enough you will
> get positive results."

My Thoughts & Feelings Today   *Date:*

Building My House

A builder who had not been able to accumulate many assets was good friends with a wealthy businessman who contracted with him to build a very nice home. Once the plans and price were agreed upon, the contractor went to work. However, because he was feeling a tight financial pinch, the builder took this opportunity to get by with inferior materials and workmanship.

When the house was finished, the builder presented the keys to his wealthy friend. Instead of taking the keys, the businessman explained that he wanted to give the house to the contractor because of their cherished friendship. "John, you have built this house especially for me, but I know you have poured yourself into it," he said. "So now I want to give it back to you free and clear."

Can you imagine the thoughts and feelings that must have been running through the mind of the contractor? To think that he had skimped and cheated on the very house that was to become his own!

The Bible encourages the followers of Christ to do good work for their employers—regardless of whether they like them or not (Ephesians 6:5-8). In fact, it says that we are to see our work being done not just for someone who gives us a paycheck, but for the Lord Himself. The next time you find yourself grumbling because your boss asked you to do some menial job, imagine that you are doing the work for God. When we begin to look at our employment in that light, we will always give it our best materials and workmanship. ♥

Inside My Open Heart...

My Thoughts & Feelings Today   Date:

"...we are to see our work being done not just for... a paycheck, but for the Lord Himself."

My Thoughts & Feelings Today   Date:

A Tasty Jar
Of Flour?

How many of you remember **waking to the smell of freshly baked biscuits in your mother's kitchen** or walking into Grandma's house and sensing the unmistakable aroma of her baking skills at work?

Did you ever stop to think about some of the ingredients that went into those tasty morsels? If you did, you probably wondered how things could end up with such a fabulous taste.

I don't know of anyone who clamors to sit down and eat a jar of flour, or begs for the shortening can and a spoon, or bursts through the front door after school and pleads for a can of baking powder. No, when you stop to consider the various ingredients that go into making biscuits, few if any of them taste very good. Only when they are together in the proper proportions can they make an incredibly delicious delight.

Life is something like that. Many things that happen to us are not very appetizing by themselves. We would rather do without them. However, the all wise God knows how to take a little bit of this and a little bit of that and mix it in with just the right proportions so that it turns into something wonderful. The Bible says that God is able to make everything turn out good for those who love Him. The individual components—experienced by themselves—may not be very tasty, but together they create a taste and aroma pleasing to us, to God and others. ♥

Inside My Open Heart...

My Thoughts & Feelings Today   *Date:*

"Many things that happen to us
are not very appetizing
by themselves."

My Thoughts & Feelings Today   *Date:*

True Beauty

Former Harvard University President Charles William Eliot (1834-1926) was born with a sizeable birthmark on his face. One can only imagine the difficulties the young man faced as he struggled with this noticeable blemish. The birthmark was the first thing people noticed when they met him.

Doctors were consulted to see what could be done surgically, but no help was available at that time. He would just have to live with it.

His mother's heart ached for her son and what he had to go through. She knew that children could be cruel and life could be hard for him. She could not remove the mark, but she wanted to help her son in some way.

Eliot's mother decided to help him rise above his misfortune. If he couldn't get rid of the misplaced mark, he would have to do his best to overcome it. She reminded him that "It's possible, with God's help, to grow a mind and a soul so big that people will forget to look at your face."

It is in the inner person where true beauty resides. Americans spend millions of dollars annually to improve their outward appearance, while often neglecting the internal person that truly makes one attractive. We can all think of someone who has the outward features associated with beauty, but yet their spirit casts an ugly hue over their being. Physical beauty is only part of the equation. To complete the package we must also develop the inner person. We need to develop such a big soul that people forget to look at our face. ♥

Inside My Open Heart...

My Thoughts & Feelings Today   *Date:*

"We need to develop such a
big soul that people forget
to look at our face."

My Thoughts & Feelings Today   *Date:*

Beautiful But Deadly

Deadly things do not always come wrapped up in ugly packages. In fact, they often appear attractive to the beholder.

A policeman was called out after a storm to patrol an area where trees were covered with ice and electric lines were broken. The sparking power lines sent prisms of multicolored light reflecting off the branches of the trees. The glow produced a rainbow of colors that was absolutely beautiful. However, the policeman's job was to keep people away from this beautiful, but deadly scene.

When John Belushi died of an overdose of cocaine and heroin, *U.S. News and World Report* wrote about the seductive dangers of cocaine, "It can do you no harm and it can drive you insane; it can give you status in society and it can wreck your career; it can make you the life of the party and it can turn you into a loner; it can be an elixir for high living and a potion for death."

The Bible often describes sin as being beautiful, but deadly. Moses was aware that the wrong things he could have done were often enjoyable—at least for a little while. However, Moses wanted to please God and gave up the pleasures of sin.

Many people have made pleasure the prime factor in determining right and wrong— not consequences or moral absolutes. Now our society is beginning to reap the whirlwind of unbridled passion for pleasure. We must remember that some things may be beautiful and deadly all at the same time. ♥

Inside My Open Heart...

My Thoughts & Feelings Today   *Date:*

"Now our society is beginning to reap the whirlwind of unbridled passion for pleasure."

My Thoughts & Feelings Today   *Date:*

Sixteen New Cars

A rather shabbily dressed man walked into a car showroom in Bodo, Norway and wanted to know if the dealership had sixteen cars of the same model on hand. The salesman sized the man up by his appearance and strange request and decided he was a smart aleck. As the salesman walked away he told the man, "I've no time for jokes, Mister! Buzz off!"

The car shopper walked out the door and crossed the street to a similar establishment, where he was greeted cordially by one of the sales staff. He gave the same request for sixteen cars of all the same model. The salesman got busy on the project and was able to come up with all the cars desired. The deal was signed and the man purchased all the automobiles—worth thousands of dollars.

The shopper represented a group of sailors who had caught a record amount of herring. The sailors had decided to buy new cars with their earnings and felt they could all do better if they bought in volume. The shabbily dressed man was sent to negotiate the deal. You might say the second salesman had a record catch of his own by not prejudging the person because of what he wore or his strange request.

When the prophet Samuel was instructed to anoint King David, Samuel was told by God that David might not look like the one "most likely to succeed." However, that was not to sway his judgment. Samuel was then reminded that, "Man looks at the outward appearance, but the Lord looks at the heart" (1 Samuel 16:7). ♥

Inside My Open Heart...

My Thoughts & Feelings Today   *Date:*

"Man looks at the outward appearance, but the Lord looks at the heart." *(1 Samuel 16:7)*

My Thoughts & Feelings Today   *Date:*

When No One Listens

The story is told of a little country boy who wore a thin, ragged coat and worn-out shoes. One bitterly cold morning he was struggling through deep snow on his way to school.

Several large youths who walked nearby began taunting him: "You call yourself a Christian? Well, then, why doesn't your God tell someone to give you a warm coat and some boots?" The lad replied, "I think He has, but no one is listening."

Our care of the needy is of great concern to God. Jesus talked often of feeding the hungry and clothing the poor. The Apostle John even challenged a person's commitment to God if that person had the means to help a needy person but refused to do it.

Jesus didn't teach indiscriminate welfare but He did teach love and compassion for those who are not able to help themselves. He never wanted us to just live for ourselves but for others and Him. The needy "others" are never to be out of our minds even if we are able to keep them out of our sight. When Jesus said we would always have the poor with us He intended that we would do what we can to help meet their needs.

Is God speaking to one of you about providing some needed hats, coats, boots or shoes? Are you listening? You may be the "angel in disguise" God wants to use us to meet the need of someone else. ♥

Inside My Open Heart...

My Thoughts & Feelings Today   *Date:*

"You may be the 'angel in disguise' God wants to use to meet the need of someone else."

My Thoughts & Feelings Today   *Date:*

Looking For Gold

Andrew Carnegie became the largest steel manufacturer in the United States, but he didn't start out that way. He came to America from Scotland as a small boy and began working at a variety of jobs. From these small jobs he moved up to become the great steel industrialist.

Part of his success was the number of others who also became rich by working for him. At one time he reportedly had at least 43 millionaires under his employment. When asked how he had hired that many wealthy men he replied that none of them were millionaires before they started to work for him. If these men were not wealthy before they were hired, how had Carnegie developed them to be such valuable and successful businessmen in his company? Carnegie replied that developing men and mining for gold are very similar. He said, "When gold is mined, several tons of dirt must be moved to get an ounce of gold; but one doesn't go into the mine looking for dirt—one goes in looking for gold."

If we are looking for the gold in others, then their worth will be the focus of our attention and talk. The dirt surrounding the gold will only be a slight hindrance and not worth discussing. I want my objective to be finding the gold in others, not talking about all the dirt that surrounds the gold. ♥

Inside My Open Heart...

My Thoughts & Feelings Today   *Date:*

"If we are looking for the gold in others, then their worth will be the focus of our attention..."

My Thoughts & Feelings Today   *Date:*

With X-ray Vision

When I was a youngster, some shoe stores had X-ray machines that showed buyers the outline of their feet within a pair of shoes. The machine stood about four feet high with a six-inch step in front of it. I would stand on the step and insert my feet through two openings and then press my face against the viewer to see my feet. There were similar viewers on the other side of the machine for my mother and the sales clerk to examine the fit.

Recently I was in prayer about a burden that was heavy on my heart. I was having a difficult time forming the thoughts in my mind that expressed the feelings boiling in my heart. I was feeling frustrated. Finally I said to the Lord, "You know my heart, look into it and see my burden." It was then that the memory of the shoe store X-ray machine came to me.

My mother, the sales clerk and I would peer into the X-ray machine and make a judgement about a pair of shoes. I envisioned God the Father looking into my heart in a similar manner to clearly see the need within me. I could almost hear Him giving instructions that represented the answer to my need. I felt the peace of God, not because the situation had changed, but because the God that loves and understands me was supplying the answer I needed.

There is nothing hidden from God, nor is there anything beyond his reach. Trust Him to see and provide the fitting answer. ♥

Inside My Open Heart...

My Thoughts & Feelings Today   *Date:*

"Trust Him to see and provide the fitting answer."

My Thoughts & Feelings Today   *Date:*

Locked Horns Signal Trouble

I n an old monastery near Babenhause, Germany, there are two pairs of deer antlers permanently interlocked. They were found in that position many years ago. One can only imagine the ramming, butting and fighting of the two animals that previously wore those antlers. Their fierce desire to be number one and get their own way ultimately cost them their lives.

Wouldn't it be something to take those interlocked antlers into every home and talk about what can happen when husbands and wives "lock horns" over things that may not really matter. What if those antlers hung in the foyer of every church that has the propensity to fight over the color of the pews or who will arrange the flowers on the altar or who will chair this year's special committee? It might not even be a bad idea to hang the antlers somewhere in the halls of Congress.

The Bible says, "A hot-tempered man stirs up dissension, but a patient man calms a quarrel" (Proverbs 15:18). I suppose we have no way of knowing how many marriages, churches, clubs or businesses could have been saved if at least one of the opposing sides had been able to step back and calm the situation. We need to work harder at finding a solution than at fighting. What a tragedy it would be for them to have to hang our interlocked antlers for all to see. ♥

Inside My Open Heart...

My Thoughts & Feelings Today   *Date:*

"We need to work harder at finding a solution than at fighting."

My Thoughts & Feelings Today   *Date:*

Protecting The Ones We Love

We are a nation determined to protect our possessions from fire, theft, and the unscrupulous. There is a device to install in your home that allows you to call a particular number from a computer and look into and listen in on your house. There's also a gadget that auto dials your pager when someone rings your doorbell. You call a preassigned number and are able to use the speaker phone at the front door as if you were inside. And then, there's a tracking sensor that can be installed in your car that allows you to be monitored by satellite anywhere in the world. You can also use the device to dial 911.

As if that weren't enough, you can buy a special apparatus that connects to your television to block out certain channels and viewing times. Other protective equipment for your computer will block out certain programs when your kids use a modem.

All this protection may be good and valuable, but there is nothing that beats having Mom or Dad accessible to children during most of their waking hours. Our children are our prized possessions. There is nothing in our lives that is more important. Spending time with them, helping them develop a good value system, providing words of encouragement, correcting and disciplining them when necessary, and giving opportunity for a strong spiritual foundation is one of the best protection systems we can provide. Our hands-on involvement with them is absolutely critical. ♥

Inside My Open Heart...

My Thoughts & Feelings Today   Date:

"...nothing beats having Mom or Dad accessible to the children..."

My Thoughts & Feelings Today   Date:

True Freedom

How many times have we heard it said that "People used to just shake hands and that settled the deal" or "When a man gave his word, that was enough." What has happened to those days? Reams of legal papers and hours of litigation now seem to be the norm.

Booker T. Washington in his book *Up From Slavery* describes how an ex-slave from Virginia felt compelled to keep his promise. Several years before Abraham Lincoln signed the Emancipation Proclamation, this slave made a contract with his owner in which the slave was permitted to buy his body back. Furthermore, the slave was permitted to work for whomever would pay the higher wages for his services. He found that he could make higher wages in Ohio. Every year the slave paid so much for his personal freedom.

Part way through his "personal buy out," the Emancipation Proclamation was signed—freeing all slaves from their obligation to former owners. Legally, the slave owed nothing more. The contract had become null and void. Yet, the slave continued to pay the amount agreed upon. He walked a large portion of the way back to Virginia and put the last payment with interest in the hand of his former owner. Why would he do this? Didn't he know it was unnecessary? In talking about the matter to Mr. Washington, the ex-slave admitted that legally he didn't have to pay the amount back. However, he had given his word and his word was something he had never broken. True freedom came when he fulfilled his promise. ♥

Inside My Open Heart...

My Thoughts & Feelings Today   *Date:*

"He had given his word and his word was something he had never broken."

My Thoughts & Feelings Today   *Date:*

All Those Idiots!

Are you easily irritated and set off by situations you encounter? Do you mumble, fret and strike out at people verbally? Do you really mean the things you say in those situations, or is it only a way of venting your frustration? Have you ever listened to what you sound like to others?

George Sweeting in the book, *Catch the Spirit of Love,* tells the story about a boy who went riding with his father—a man who drove with little regard for anyone. "He fussed and fumed, bellowed and shouted at the other drivers as he drove through town. Finally they arrived home. Later that day, the boy went out in the car with his mother. As they drove peacefully along, the boy asked, 'Mom, where are all the idiots?' 'Idiots?' his mother asked, puzzled. 'Yes. This morning when I was out with Daddy we saw seven of them!'"

I wonder if the father ever thought about the impression he was leaving with his young son? Did he ever consider what his attitude was saying about respect for others?

Learning to manage ourselves during stressful times is extremely important for successful living. Life can be frustrating at times, leaving us tense and upset. But, how we handle ourselves during the difficult times says much about our character and how much personal control we have. The writer of the Proverbs put it this way: "Better a patient man than a warrior, a man who controls his temper than one who takes a city (16:32). ♥

Inside My Open Heart...

My Thoughts & Feelings Today   *Date:*

"Learning to manage ourselves during stressful times is extremely important..."

My Thoughts & Feelings Today   *Date:*

Vow Of Silence

I n his book *21 Unbreakable Laws of Life,* **Max Anders describes a man who was unhappy with just about everything—his family, his work and life in general.** He wanted to get away from it all and decided to join a monastery where silence was law. Only two words could be spoken every five years.

He felt his search for happiness was finally over. He thought he had found what he had been looking for. There would be no stress, no one to bother him—complete silence.

At the end of his first five years he was brought in before his superior who said, "You have two words which you can speak. Would you like to say anything?"

The man motioned that he did and said, "Bad food!"

At the end of the next five years of silence, he was again given the opportunity to speak two words to his superior. His carefully chosen words this time were, "Hard bed!"

As he ended his third five-year period of silence, he was again given the opportunity to speak two words. This time he said "I quit."

His superior responded, "Well, I'm not surprised. You've done nothing but complain since you got here!"

When our sole pursuit is finding happiness, we are usually disappointed. Happiness is not a stand alone commodity. It is found in our pursuit of things more noble. True happiness is a result of pursuing God. ♥

Inside My Open Heart...

My Thoughts & Feelings Today   *Date:*

"When our sole pursuit is finding happiness, we are usually disappointed."

My Thoughts & Feelings Today   *Date:*

You Have It!

The great Harvard psychologist, William James, was known for his famous "as if" principle. The theory was that "If you wish to possess a qualification or an emotion, act as if you already had it." Picture and feel yourself in possession of it. Let it possess your being. For example, "If you need to be courageous then act "as if" you already were courageous. Shakespeare said, "Assume a virtue if you have it not."

Faith is one of those virtues that is important for us to cultivate. Jesus talked often about the importance of faith in our daily lives. He said things like, "According to your faith it will be done..." (Matthew 9:29) and "If you have faith as small as a mustard seed seemingly impossible things can happen" (Matthew 17:20). A mustard seed is about the size of a small grape seed. I had a friend who often said, "it doesn't take much faith, but what faith you have needs to be like pure mustard."

Faith by itself is not sufficient. Our faith must be based on God's faithfulness in doing what He promised. Repeatedly the Bible speaks of the God who cannot lie and who has fulfilled all He said He would do. In the light of this truth, Jesus said, "Have faith in God" (Mark 11:22). ♥

Inside My Open Heart...

My Thoughts & Feelings Today   *Date:*

"Faith is one of those virtues
that is important for us
to cultivate."

My Thoughts & Feelings Today   *Date:*

Jump In Faith

Donner Atwood in *Reformed Review* relates the story of a father and son who were fleeing from a building **being bombed during WWII.** The father quickly leaped into a bomb crater in front of their home. The son paused on the edge of the large hole, afraid to proceed farther because of the darkness. His father called to him to jump, but fear gripped him. The boy responded, "Dad, I can't see you."

The burning buildings in the background created a silhouette of the little boy that the father could clearly see. As the father looked up he yelled to his boy, "But, I can see you. Jump!" The boy went ahead and jumped out of simple trust into the arms of his waiting father. He couldn't see his father, but he trusted him.

In a similar way, God asks us to trust Him. He instructs us to give when we think we ought to be keeping for ourselves. Our reasoning is that we will never have enough if we give to someone else. The writer of the Proverbs says, "One man gives freely, yet gains even more;" (Proverbs 11:24). We don't see how someone can keep giving away and yet gain even more, but that's what God wants us to do. God says, "Jump. Just try Me."

The Bible also says, "A generous man will prosper; he who refreshes others will himself be refreshed" (Proverbs 11:25). If you have been hoarding your life because you didn't think you had enough to share with others, why not take a big jump of faith and give freely to someone else? ♥

Inside My Open Heart...

My Thoughts & Feelings Today   *Date:*

"...God asks us to trust Him...to give when we think we ought to be keeping for ourselves..."

My Thoughts & Feelings Today   *Date:*

Skills Of Defense

In the movie *Karate Kid,* young Daniel asks Mister Miagi to teach him karate. Miagi agrees—on the condition that Daniel does not question his methods of instruction.

Daniel shows up the next day, eager to learn. Rather than some great lesson, Mister Miagi has him paint a fence—using precise up and down motions. Then, Mr. Miagi demonstrates the stroke for Daniel to use when scrubbing the deck. Daniel wonders what these things have to do with karate, but he says nothing.

Next, Miagi explains the stroke he wants Daniel to use for washing and waxing three weather-beaten cars. Daniel reaches his limit: "I thought you were going to teach me karate, but all I have done is your unwanted chores!"

The old man's face is flushed with anger and he says, "I *have* been teaching you karate! Defend yourself!"

Miagi thrusts his arm at Daniel, who instinctively defends himself with an arm motion exactly like that used in one of his chores. Miagi follows up with a strong kick, and again Daniel diverts the blow with a motion used in his chores. After several similar exchanges, Miagi simply walks away. He allows Daniel to discover for himself that the mundane and repetitive actions of his chores helped him develop his defense skills.

In a similar way, the repetitive acts of Godly living prepare us to instinctively act when confronted by an attack to compromise our principles and morals. The Bible says, "do not grow weary in doing good." ♥

Inside My Open Heart...

My Thoughts & Feelings Today   Date:

"...the repetitive acts of Godly
living and thinking prepare us to
instinctively act..."

My Thoughts & Feelings Today   Date:

An Act Of Friendship

t wasn't easy for Jackie Robinson to break into major league baseball. While breaking the color barrier Robinson had to endure the jeering of crowds in nearly every major league park.

One day while fielding a ground ball in his home park in Brooklyn, he committed an error. His own fans began to jeer him. He felt humiliated. He stood at second base shocked at what he was hearing. At that moment, "Pee Wee" Reese, the Brooklyn shortstop, came over and stood next to him. Then in a courageous act of friendship, Reese put his arm around Robinson's shoulder and faced the crowd. A hush settled over the stadium. Robinson later commented that this act of friendship saved his career.

Sometimes we find people to be fair-weather friends. They stick around when things are going nicely but when adversity strikes or they are asked to help, they disappear. False friends have often been compared to your shadow. As long as there is sunshine, it sticks close by. But the minute you step into the shade, it disappears."

The Bible says, "A friend loves at all times, and a brother is born for adversity" (Proverbs 17:17). A true friend is the first person who comes in when the whole world has gone out. There may be a person near you who is praying that God would send a friend who will put an arm around the shoulder and face the jeering crowds with them. Wouldn't you like to be that friend? ♥

Inside My Open Heart...

My Thoughts & Feelings Today   *Date:*

"...a true friend is the first person who comes in when the whole world has gone out."

My Thoughts & Feelings Today   *Date:*

Looking Good

Our yard had been chewed up by animals and dried up from lack of water. After a great deal of hard work, things were beginning to look pretty good. When I mentioned this to the golf club manager who had helped advise us on the project, he said "It's a good 30-mile-per-hour yard—it doesn't look too bad when you're driving by it at 30 miles per hour."

How often are our lives like that? How often do we want to keep people at arms' length because we don't want them to see the real us? Things don't look too bad from 30 miles per hour, but don't look too closely. Such an attitude may be caused by inferiority feelings. We see ourselves like a dime store ring among priceless jewelry. We simply don't feel we are good enough. On the other hand we may not want others to look too closely because we are trying to be something we are not. We are afraid that close observation by others will reveal the facade we are living behind.

How much better to just be who we are rather than try to appear bigger and better than life. We don't have to put on a facade or cover up to impress people. We need to learn to be satisfied with the person God made us and what we have become. If there are areas that we wish were different then we can work to change them. But let's not hide behind a life that only looks good when people go by it at a high rate of speed. Let's be honest and transparent with ourselves and others. ♥

Inside My Open Heart...

My Thoughts & Feelings Today   *Date:*

"...just be who we are rather than try to appear bigger and better than life."

My Thoughts & Feelings Today   *Date:*

I'm Gonna Get To It

Acommon delay tactic we use to avoid things we should do is the saying "I'm gonna get to it one of these days." Often, we say this to help us feel good about our intentions or to get a spouse, parent or friend to keep from nagging us.

In the book *Uncommon Friends*, James Newton tells a story about Henry Ford's response to a procrastinating staff. Concerned about the fenders on one of his company's cars, he had instructed the engineering department to make certain changes. Several weeks went by, but no changes had been made. He was told they had not been able to work out the problems.

One day Ford showed up at the plant unannounced and directed the presses to be stopped. He told two mechanics to take the molds being used to stamp out the old fenders and put them on the floor. He told them to "Get your sledgehammers and break each one of them." Then he turned and walked out. Within two days the presses were again running—with new molds that had been made faster than previously thought possible.

We too can change. We don't have to delay. God wants to help us. The changes we think will take a long time can be made easier and faster than we thought possible. Be determined. Start right now to change (e.g., improve your marriage, increase your education, spend more time with your family, or make a commitment to serve God). Don't end the year still saying, "I'm gonna get to it one of these days." ♥

Inside My Open Heart...

My Thoughts & Feelings Today   *Date:*

"Don't end the year still saying,
'I'm gonna get to it one
of these days.'"

My Thoughts & Feelings Today   *Date:*

Courage & Compassion

One of the founders of the Salvation Army, Mary Booth tells a story from her childhood that teaches an important lesson about compassion.

Mary remembers seeing a man dragged away to prison by an officer of the law. The large crowd that had gathered began to laugh and make fun of the unfortunate man. Her heart immediately went out to him. It seemed he had no one to befriend him. He was alone in the world.

Immediately she began to walk beside him. She was determined that the prisoner would know that—even if he suffered because of his own actions—he would have a friend in her.

Our response to hurting people shouldn't be based on how it will affect our reputation. We shouldn't consider whether or not contact will benefit us or if they are worthy of our help. Following the Watergate scandal, Billy Graham was asked if his association with the late President Nixon would damage his reputation. Dr. Graham responded that he was a friend of President Nixon before Watergate and would continue to be his friend.

Jesus respectfully befriended the needy. When an adulteress was dragged before him by leaders who had no compassion for the lady and no respect for Jesus, he told her that "Neither do I condemn you. Go now and leave your life of sin" (John 8:11).

There may be someone today who is shunned by others and needs someone to walk alongside them. Do you have the courage and compassion to be their friend? ♥

Inside My Open Heart...

My Thoughts & Feelings Today   *Date:*

"Our response to hurting people shouldn't be based on how it will affect our reputation."

My Thoughts & Feelings Today   *Date:*

Things Just Rub Off

More than just a cute little phrase that someone thought up, "like father like son" is true more times than not. It's difficult to live in the same home with someone for 18-20 years during the most formative time in one's life and not be affected. Things just rub off. Many of the characteristics we carry into our adult life were absorbed by just being around our parents. It wasn't just what they taught, but what we observed when they didn't even realize it.

A teenage boy came home from school with a note from the teacher stating that she had to discipline the boy for swearing. When the father pressed the boy for an explanation, he admitted it was just like the teacher said. She had taken him out into the hall to talk with him and asked him where he had learned such awful language. At this point in the story the son said, "But I covered for you dad. I told her I had learned it from the parrot."

A sign was posted on the golf course side of a private fence. The sign said, **"Attention Golfers! We are raising small children behind this fence, so please refrain from enlarging their vocabularies. Thank you!"**

Our attitudes, language, demeanor, and values are often more easily caught than taught. Children observe, and then mimic what we model. Jesus reminds adults that they have a great responsibility in the proper training and care of children. ♥

Inside My Open Heart...

My Thoughts & Feelings Today   *Date:*

"Our attitudes, language, demeanor, and values are often more easily caught than taught."

My Thoughts & Feelings Today   *Date:*

Do You Push Or Pull?

A frazzled looking and out of breath man frantically asked some bystanders if they had seen a certain group of people pass by. When asked why he was looking for them, he explained that he was their leader.

Here was a man given the title of leader who wasn't truly leading. He may have had all the right education and even started out with his group, but something happened before they got very far. Someone has said that if we say we are a leader, but no one is following— we are just taking a long walk.

A leader needs to be far enough in front of the group to set the course, but near enough to remain in sight.

What a leader instinctively knows is that it's easier to lead a group than it is drive them. General Eisenhower frequently demonstrated this principle by using a piece of string as an illustration. He would place the string on a table and say, "Pull it and it'll follow wherever you wish. Push it and it will go nowhere at all."

A leader also cares about those whom he leads. A man was observed beating the flock of sheep he was driving across a field. The observer questioned, "I thought shepherds led their sheep?" The man said, "I'm not the shepherd; I'm the butcher."

Leadership is extremely important, but it is not easy. It requires skill, patience and compassion. If any three of the ingredients are missing, true leadership becomes almost impossible. ♥

Inside My Open Heart...

My Thoughts & Feelings Today   Date:

"...if we say we are a leader, but no one is following—we are just taking a long walk."

My Thoughts & Feelings Today   Date:

Paid With A Glass Of Milk

During the summer holidays while in medical school, Dr. Howard A. Kelly sold books to help with expenses. He is a renowned physician and surgeon and devout practicing Christian.

During one of those Summer days, he became thirsty and stopped at a farmhouse for a glass of water. A girl came to the door and kindly responded that she would gladly pour him a glass of milk—if he wished. For a long time, he remembered how the cool milk was *so* refreshing!

Years passed and Dr. Kelly graduated from medical school and became the chief surgeon at John Hopkins Hospital. One day, a seriously ill patient was admitted from a rural area. She was given special care and placed in a private room with a private nurse. The skilled chief surgeon spared no effort to make the patient well. After undergoing surgery, she convalesced rapidly.

One day, she was told by the head nurse that "tomorrow you will go home!" Though her joy was great, it was somewhat lessened by the thought of the large bill she must owe the hospital and surgeon. With a heavy heart, she began to read the itemized statement from the top down. She sighed. But as her eyes lowered, she saw the following notation at the bottom of the large bill: "Paid in full with one glass of milk!" It was signed Howard A. Kelly, MD.

Your act of kindness may not result in a similar action, but it will not go unnoticed by our Heavenly Father. He makes note of even a cup of cold water given in His name. ♥

Inside My Open Heart...

My Thoughts & Feelings Today   Date:

"Your act of kindness...
will not go unnoticed by
our Heavenly Father."

My Thoughts & Feelings Today   Date:

Unique & Rare

An unusual auction took place on December 2, 1995 at Phillip's Fine Art Auctioneers in New York. Among the hundreds of items auctioned were a Moon rock brought back by Apollo 12, a sliver of Mars from the Zagami meteorite that fell to earth in 1962 in Nigeria, the Galaxy Opal (the world's largest at 3,749 carats), a complete skeleton of an ice-age cave bear, the nests of two Theropod dinosaur eggs (each eighteen inches long and six inches wide), and a rare piece of amber that contained a whole kiwi-like fruit from the Oligocene era.

A desire to own something unique and rare motivates certain people. They like to add it to their list of possessions.

When we moved from Ohio to Michigan many years ago, our only possessions were our car, furniture and other personal belongings. I can still remember how I felt when all we owned was easily packed into our hatch back car and the front 25% of the moving van. That was all we had—not very impressive. My wife and I couldn't help but stop and think about what was most important. Our prized possessions were all in the car: our two children, each other, our wedding album and a few other keepsakes. A similar realization would be true for most of you, if you took the time to analyze it.

We need to be constantly reminded to devote our energy to that which is most important. Rather than pursuing a rare piece from an auction, we need to focus our attention on those things that will outlive us. ♥

Inside My Open Heart...

My Thoughts & Feelings Today   *Date:*

"...we need to focus our
attention on those things
that will outlive us."

My Thoughts & Feelings Today   *Date:*

Another Meal Together

A young newly ordained preacher was invited to speak to a small Missouri congregation many years ago. Being poor, the young preacher had to walk the 20 miles to his assignment. He arrived tired and hungry. During his message he stumbled and stammered—often losing his train of thought. Needless to say, he did not make a very favorable showing.

The congregation, unaware of his hunger and exhaustion from the long trek over the back-country roads, was harsh in its judgment of him as a preacher. No one invited him to dinner. Dejected he started his long lonely walk back home. A black janitor who lived in a crude shanty nearby, saw him and invited the young man to share his meal.

Years later, that young preacher became a widely known and respected bishop. He was invited to dedicate a new church on the site where he'd been unkindly treated years before.

After the service, many invited the Bishop for dinner, but he turned them all down. Instead, he chose to celebrate the occasion by eating with the elderly black janitor who had been so kind to him years before.

Who we help should not be determined by the person's status in society. According to the Bible, kindness and compassion should be part of our everyday living (Colossians 3:12).

William Penn said, "I expect to pass through life but once. If therefore, there be any kindness I can show, or any good thing I can do to any fellow human being, let me do it now, and not defer or neglect it, as I shall not pass this way again." ♥

Inside My Open Heart...

My Thoughts & Feelings Today   Date:

"Who we help should not be determined by the person's status in society."

My Thoughts & Feelings Today   Date:

Moving In To Make A Point

While Jane Byrne was Mayor of Chicago, there was a rash of gang-related slayings in one of the large inner-city housing projects. Efforts to curb the violence by law enforcement agencies proved difficult at best and basically ineffective.

Then a decision was made that surprised even the most seasoned political observers. Mayor Byrne announced that she and her husband were moving into the apartment complex. Even her critics agreed that this was a bold initiative that was bound to bring about some of the desired results.

The outcome of her decision was that crime was indeed reduced in the targeted area and a new sense of pride and hope swept over the community.

We may question why the Mayor and her family needed to sacrifice their comfortable surroundings to move to a crime infected area. After all, they were the first family. They got the perks. True leadership, however, has its price to pay. Many times people only see the benefits that leaders receive—not the tremendous sacrifice that goes with the responsibility.

Jesus reminds us that much is required from the one who has been given much. A position of leadership is not just for the perks one may feel entitled to. It is a position of service to the body one is called to lead. If you have had the mantle of leadership thrust around your shoulders, wear it proudly, but also as a sacred trust. ♥

Inside My Open Heart...

My Thoughts & Feelings Today   *Date:*

"True leadership, however, has its price to pay."

My Thoughts & Feelings Today   *Date:*

With Great Potential

In a large city there was a man who opened a delicatessen on a street that already had two salami salons. One advertised bologna that was the "finest in the world." The second claimed to be the "best in the universe."

The new man on the block simply declared "nicest in the neighborhood." He backed it up with thoughtful courteous service that went far beyond the norm. That man used the gift of "kindness" and his business far exceeded its potential.

Charles M. Schulz said that "There is no greater burden than great potential." It really demands much of us. It won't let us settle for mediocrity when it is accompanied with the determination to be the best that God created us to be.

When we look at the tremendous strides humanity has made—not only in the fields of science and technology, but in other areas as well—it is incredible. We went from the "outhouse" to "outer-space" in a few short years. Cures have been found for so many infectious diseases. People are living longer and enjoying it more. All this is possible because many people were willing to assume the burden of their potential.

We all have certain God-given gifts and talents that are uniquely ours. We may not have the scientific mind of an Albert Einstein or Louis Pasteur. We perhaps can't paint like Van Gogh, play a piano like Van Cliburn or sing like Pavarotti. But God has blessed each of us with gifts and He always provides us with opportunities to use them. ♥

Inside My Open Heart...

My Thoughts & Feelings Today   *Date:*

"God has blessed each of us with gifts and He always provides us with opportunities to use them."

My Thoughts & Feelings Today   *Date:*

Don't Fret

Stress is caused by our response to a situation, not the situation itself, according to stress management consultant Donald Tubesing. He gives this example: "If you get stuck in traffic, you can work yourself up and yell at anyone who beeps his horn. Or you can view the time you're sitting there as the only uninterrupted 15 minutes you'll have all day."

John Curtis, founder and director of the University of Wisconsin Stress Management Institute, says that he believes "90 percent of stress is brought on by not living in the present moment—worrying about what's already happened, what's going to happen, or what could happen."

Jesus didn't want people to worry all the time. He pointed out to His followers how God faithfully cared for the birds. He wanted the people to understand that they would be cared for as well, since they were more valuable. We need to see what we can do to overcome worry, since it cannot add a single hour to our lives.

God's care for his people is legendary. Many of the great Bible characters found themselves in very difficult circumstances and invariably God reminds them not to worry. "Do not fret"... "wait on the Lord" ... "do not be afraid" ... these are only a few of the phrases God used to quiet the hearts of His people. He had everything under control. He still does.

If you have been worrying and fretting over situations that you can't control, why not rest in a God who cares about you? ♥

Inside My Open Heart...

My Thoughts & Feelings Today   Date:

"We need to... overcome worry, since it cannot add a single hour to our lives."

My Thoughts & Feelings Today   Date:

Getting
The Point

Sometimes we just don't get it. As hard as someone tries to explain something, their point is not clear to us. It is a little bit like the boy at school who said to his teacher, "I ain't got no pencil."

Thinking this would be a good teaching moment, she corrected him by saying, "It's 'I don't have a pencil. You don't have a pencil. We don't have any pencils. They don't have any pencils.' Is that clear?"

The child gave her a bewildered look and said, "No... What happened to all them pencils?"

There are times when God tries to correct my attitude or my life-style, but I don't always get the point. I'm still thinking about the pencils and He has something totally different in mind.

God is interested in helping us to get the most out of life, if only we will listen. The writer of Proverbs tells us we need to be alert to God's teaching moments. He advises us to pay attention to what God is trying to say to us. He put it this way, "Don't just trust your own wisdom and intuition. If you truly want to know God's will for your life and are willing to follow it, He will direct your path" (Proverbs 3:5-6). The more you seek to know God's will the more you will understand that He's not just talking about pencils, but rather deeper things He wants you to know. ♥

Inside My Open Heart...

My Thoughts & Feelings Today   *Date:*

"God is interested in helping us to get the most out of life..."

My Thoughts & Feelings Today   *Date:*

Test Of Integrity

Dr. David Augsburger tells the true story of how young Lt. John Blanchard struck up an acquaintance with Miss Hollis Maynell. They began corresponding by mail and during the thirteen months of writing they fell in love with each other.

Finally, they arranged to meet in Grand Central Station in New York. Hollis agreed to identify herself by wearing a red rose in her lapel. As the young soldier boy anxiously waited, a young beautiful blonde-haired woman approached him. She spoke briefly to him, even asking if he was going her way. But, she was not wearing a red rose. His heart momentarily dropped. However, immediately behind the young blonde was a plump, gray-haired woman in her mid-forties, wearing a wrinkled brown coat. She was not exactly a young soldier's heart throb, but there *was* a red rose in her lapel. John felt a sense of disappointment, but he wanted to meet the woman who had stirred his heart during the past 13 months. After all, he reminded himself, "love is not dependent on beauty."

He went over to the woman and introduced himself and invited her to dinner. The woman responded, "I don't know what this is all about, son, but the young lady in the green suit who just went by begged me to wear this rose on my coat. She said if you asked me out to dinner I should tell you that she is waiting for you across the street. She said it was some kind of test."

We can only assume that John and Hollis lived happily together—John having passed the test of integrity. ♥

Inside My Open Heart...

My Thoughts & Feelings Today   Date:

**"After all, he reminded
himself, 'love is not
dependent on beauty.'"**

My Thoughts & Feelings Today   Date:

Where God Isn't

During a recent morning walk, I looked out across the waters of Lake Huron into the dark blue early morning sky and saw silhouetted a flock of geese flying to their morning feeding. I observed the familiar pattern of the flying "V" and again marvelled at how they do that. How do they know to get into that pattern? How can they all independently work together as a team to get more lift and speed to their flight? Somehow they have a God-given instinct that helps them to do the things that are necessary for their well being and survival.

The Psalmist stated that "The heavens declare the glory of God; the skies proclaim the work of His hands." The apostle Paul asserted that "God's invisible qualities—His eternal power and divine nature—have been clearly seen, being understood from what has been made, so that men are without excuse."

A small boy was walking home from school. As he meandered his way along he kicked over a rock and observed the bugs that scampered off to more protective shelter. A little farther along he stood in awe of a butterfly that winged its flight to places unknown. As he came upon some trees he saw the playful squirrels chasing one another in what looked like a game of backyard tag. Not long after this the boy came upon an older man who was an agnostic who said, "I will give you a quarter if you can show me where God is." To which the observant little boy responded, "I'll give you a dollar if you can show me where God isn't." ♥

Inside My Open Heart...

My Thoughts & Feelings Today   Date:

"I'll give you a dollar if you can show me where God isn't."

My Thoughts & Feelings Today   Date:

Humpty Dumpty

A favorite nursery rhyme goes like this: "**Humpty Dumpty sat on a wall,** Humpty Dumpty had a great fall. All the king's horses and all the king's men couldn't put Humpty together again."

According to those who know about such things, this piece of wisdom is a relic thousands of years old. Versions have appeared in eight European languages. In its primitive stages, however, Humpty Dumpty was a riddle. It asked the question: what, when broken, can never be repaired, not even by strong or wise individuals? The answer is an egg. Regardless of how hard we try, a broken egg can never be put back together again. We simply have to learn to live with the mess.

Our lives can be as fragile as an egg and sometimes they can even get as messed up. Wrong decisions, bad choices and unavoidable circumstances can turn a thing of beauty into despair. But a broken life doesn't have to stay that way. Although it's true that we cannot always put life back to its original design, when we turn the pieces over to God, He is able to bring beauty out of ashes. He has a master design for each of our lives and even when His design has been marred and scarred by our choices, He is still able to fix it. The key is to let Him put it back together.

♥

Inside My Open Heart...

My Thoughts & Feelings Today   Date:

"...even when His design has been marred and scarred by our choices, He is still able to fix it."

My Thoughts & Feelings Today   Date:

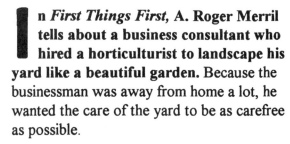

It Takes A Gardener

n *First Things First,* **A. Roger Merril tells about a business consultant who hired a horticulturist to landscape his yard like a beautiful garden.** Because the businessman was away from home a lot, he wanted the care of the yard to be as carefree as possible.

Little or no maintenance was his re-occurring theme. Automatic sprinklers and any other labor saving devices possible were to be included in the design.

Finally the designer approached the homeowner and said, "There's one thing you need to deal with before we go any further. If there's no gardener, there's no garden!"

There are some things that simply don't grow well without attention. Marriage and family relationships don't survive without a lot of personal care and nurturing. Entertaining devices like the TV are not good surrogate parents. Such things can never take the place of mom and dad interacting daily and even hourly with their children. In the same way, moms and dads need to pay close attention to their relationship with each other or the weeds of indifference, coldness and stagnation can flourish in their marriage.

It takes a lot of attention and care to cultivate the kind of family most people dream about. This family garden, when attended to regularly, does not require nearly as much work as it would if weeds were permitted to accumulate. ♥

Inside My Open Heart...

My Thoughts & Feelings Today   Date:

"It takes a lot of attention and care to cultivate the kind of family most people dream about."

My Thoughts & Feelings Today   Date:

Frustration best describes the feeling of being around undisciplined children—especially when those children belong to someone else. Most of us have at least one time been in a situation at an office, church or club and observed children who were making life miserable for everyone. But how do you get things under control without offending the parents? How do you politely say, "Quit that."

Out Of Control

While a mother was visiting a doctor's office for her new baby's check-up, her five-year-old son was making a mess of an adjoining treatment room. The mother asked the doctor if he minded her five-year-old playing in the room. "Not at all," said the doctor calmly. "He'll quiet down in a moment when he gets to the poison cabinet."

Of course, the doctor was only kidding, but in real life, undisciplined behavior often leads to reaping the results of unbridled desires.

Children and adults get along better when there is discipline. Children need to know their limits and the consequences for going beyond those limits. If we don't learn control when we are young, we are usually out of control when we are older. The Bible frequently reminds the first century Christians that one of the greatest personal attributes is self control. Parents help teach that virtue as they properly discipline their children. ♥

Inside My Open Heart...

My Thoughts & Feelings Today   *Date:*

"...undisciplined behavior often leads to reaping the results of unbridled desires."

My Thoughts & Feelings Today   *Date:*

Cheerful Hearts

Attitudes are contagious. I can think of several individuals I have visited with over the years who greatly depressed me. I learned that whenever I was going to meet with these individuals, I would have to get myself emotionally and mentally psyched-up before I made the call. Even then, I have come out dragging on several occasions.

It was not their situation that was so terrible, but the emotional attitude they possessed. If I stayed with them too long, I found their cynicism and pessimism to be contagious.

On the other hand, a positive, upbeat person can be like a breath of fresh air. It's like turning on the lights when they come into the room. There is just something about them that makes them enjoyable to be around. Their attitude lifts your spirit.

A cheerful heart is the same as giving good medicine, according to the author of Proverbs. You don't need a prescription to either give or receive this good medicine. It is contagious. You get it and give it by just being around others. There is a Bible character that must have been one of those "cheerful heart" people because he was given the name "Son of Encouragement." He evidently gave a lot of light to a dark room. Today as you greet your children, walk into the office, or take your seat in the classroom... would anyone think to call you a person of encouragement? ♥

Inside My Open Heart...

My Thoughts & Feelings Today   *Date:*

"...would anyone think to call you a person of encouragement?"

My Thoughts & Feelings Today   *Date:*

Two-Way Street

A woman was complaining to her counselor that she had been coming to him for two years and all he ever did was listen. "You never say anything back."

The counselor sat there in silence.

Finally, in desperation, she said, "I don't have to come here to get this kind of help. I can just stay home with my husband. That's all he ever does."

Lack of communication or at least poor communication is one of the greatest problems faced in marriage. The wife often wants her husband to listen... to give her his undivided attention... to act like he genuinely cares about her interests. On the other hand, what he considers "chit chat" doesn't come easily so he avoids it—especially if feelings or sentimental things are involved.

Men and women have different needs and desires and therefore have completely different ideas about communication. They get upset when the other person doesn't respond like they think they should. Frustration and anger are often the result.

What can couples do? How can they improve their communications and their marriages? Here are some suggestions:

1. Ask God for wisdom and understanding.

2. Seek to understand life through the other person's eyes. This is not easy, since we usually don't think the same way.

3. Attempt to meet the other person's need, rather than focusing only on yourself. ♥

Inside My Open Heart...

My Thoughts & Feelings Today   Date:

"Seek to understand life
through the other
person's eyes."

My Thoughts & Feelings Today   Date:

Stinky Diapers

The Bible says "As a man thinketh in his heart—so is he." In light of that, what kind of person are you?

Do you get up in the morning thinking about all the things that are wrong in your life or what is right? Are you beat down before you ever get out the door in the morning? Or do you head off to work or school with a spring in your step because you anticipate the great things that will happen that day? Do you see yourself as a failure or successful at what you do?

I often talk to young parents about the not so nice job of changing diapers. It is not always such a pleasant job, but I encourage young couples to just think about how they would feel if the plumbing wasn't working on their new little baby. Attitude can make all the difference in the world.

Have you observed someone walking stoop shouldered, slow gaited, and despondent? Didn't you want to go up to them, throw their shoulders back, quicken their step and encourage them to improve their attitude. If they would do that you knew how much better they would look and feel. To a large extent their appearance was a result of "stinkin' thinkin'."

Thinking on things that are lovely, pure, of a good report and honest was the advice the Apostle Paul gave to some of his early followers (Philippians 4:8). That's good advice for all of us. ♥

Inside My Open Heart...

My Thoughts & Feelings Today	Date:

> ## "Attitude can make all the difference in the world."

My Thoughts & Feelings Today	Date:

Feeding
The Enemy

During the 1800s, the occupying British troops were often in armed conflict with the tribes people of New Zealand. Following one particular skirmish, the British soldiers were resting on the banks of the Waikato River. The troops were short on supplies and expected the Maori warriors to attack at anytime.

Suddenly the British lookout announced that several large canoes were coming up the river. General Cameron and his men prepared for an attack—assuming that the canoes were loaded with warriors. To their surprise, the boats were filled with milk, goats and potatoes. The British were puzzled. Why was the enemy bringing them food?

The Maoris said, "We heard you were hungry, and the Book the missionaries brought us says, 'If your enemy is hungry, feed him!' You are the enemy; you are hungry; we feed you; that is all!" The Maoris quickly unloaded the goods and left.

Much of the thinking today focuses on "how can I get back at a person." It is summed up in the phrase, "Don't get mad—get even." Many people do both: get mad and try to get even.

Showing kindness to our enemy is difficult and unpopular, but it is Biblical. Rather than seeking revenge on the person whom we feel has wronged us, we are to demonstrate mercy.

Does such action seem unreasonable to you? Why not ask God to help you try it? Your situation will no doubt improve and God also promises to reward you (Proverbs 25:22). ♥

Inside My Open Heart...

My Thoughts & Feelings Today   *Date:*

"Showing kindness to our enemy is difficult and unpopular, but it is Biblical."

My Thoughts & Feelings Today   *Date:*

Daddy's At The Helm

Mariane Uhlig, a German missionary, was sailing on a ship from America to Japan. She struck up a conversation with the Captain of the ship who shared her religious interests and convictions. She inquired as to how he had come to have so much faith and trust.

He related how years before he had invited his wife and young (8-or-9-year-old) daughter to go on one of the voyages. Just as now, it was a very stormy trip. In fact things got so bad that he had given orders for all hands to be on deck and had lowered the life boats.

Everyone was already on deck, but his young daughter was still asleep in the cabin. Her mother woke her and said, "Get up quickly. There is a storm and the boat is in danger of sinking!" The little one looked at her mother and said: "Mommy, is Daddy at the helm?" She was told he was. She replied, "Then everything will be all right!" With that she turned over and fell asleep again.

As the father considered his daughter's response, he wondered why he couldn't have that much trust in his heavenly Father. Why did he have to fret and stew and worry about the eventual outcome of the storms of life? With God at the helm, everything would be all right.

Today, why not picture yourself laying all of your burdens, fears and worries at the feet of your heavenly Father and then trust Him. ♥

Inside My Open Heart...

My Thoughts & Feelings Today   Date:

"Why... fret and stew and worry about the eventual outcome of the storms of life?"

My Thoughts & Feelings Today   Date:

Facing The Storms In Life

Buckner Fanning tells the story of a pastor friend who developed a heart problem that left him tired and unable to function as a pastor. His doctors gave him little hope about either the quality or quantity of his life.

In frustration he went to another specialist for a second opinion. After a long and rigorous examination, the doctor assured the pastor that he could be helped. After surgery was performed and recovery completed, the pastor returned to his church with new enthusiasm. During a follow-up visit, the pastor thanked the doctor again and again for returning both quantity and quality to his life. The doctor said, "I have had a part in helping you go on living, but the quality of life is now up to you."

All of us will face the storms in life. God has promised to be with His children in and through the storms. The question we often ask is, "Will there be quality in my life? Will trials make me bitter or better, depressed or determined, soured or strengthened?"

Perhaps the best question that can be asked is not why did this thing happen, but what can I become because of it? The Bible says, "And we know that in all things God works for the good of those who love him, who have been called according to his purpose" (Romans 8:28). ♥

Inside My Open Heart...

My Thoughts & Feelings Today   *Date:*

"Will trials make me bitter or better, depressed or determined..."

My Thoughts & Feelings Today   *Date:*

Staying On Course

Most of us have heard of Murphy's Law—"If anything can go wrong, it will"—but there are others. Here are a few that you may have also heard:

■ "Negative expectations yield negative results. Positive expectations yield negative results."

■ "The other line always moves faster."

■ "The chance of the bread falling with the buttered side down is directly proportional to the cost of the carpet."

■ "When in doubt, mumble."

■ "Inside every large problem is a small problem struggling to get out."

Two turtles were crossing a busy freeway. The first turtle stayed on his course, believing that despite all the obstacles he had to overcome, despite not knowing what was coming next, he would make it to the other side. He refused to be guided by Murphy's Law. He knew things could be better.

The second turtle became frightened halfway across the road and retreated into his shell, saying, "I knew all along I wouldn't make it. I never should have started this journey. If something can go wrong, it will. I'm finished." And his prophecy was self-fulfilling.

Do you sometimes live your life like that? Are you fearful to move because it might be the wrong move or something bad might happen? God calls on us to stay on course, to keep the faith even when times are difficult. God calls us to stay out of our shells, so that we might experience victory. ♥

Inside My Open Heart...

My Thoughts & Feelings Today   Date:

"Are you fearful to move because it might be the wrong move..."

My Thoughts & Feelings Today   Date:

Priorities

Billionaire H. Ross Perot was quoted in Fortune magazine: "Guys, just remember, if you get real lucky, if you make a lot of money, if you go out and buy a lot of stuff—it's gonna break. You got your biggest, fanciest mansion in the world. It has air conditioning. It's got a pool. Just think of all the pumps that are going to go out. Or go to a yacht basin any place in the world. Nobody is smiling, and I'll tell you why. Something broke that morning. The generator's out; the microwave oven doesn't work....Things just don't mean happiness."

Kerrin-Lee Gartner of Calgary, Alberta was an immediate sensation in 1992 when she became the first Canadian in history to win Olympic gold in the women's downhill. Shortly after her victory, an announcer interviewing her commented that this must surely be the most significant day of her life. "No," she replied. "The most significant day was the day of my marriage—but this ranks pretty high." Even the greatest of achievements cannot compare with the greatest relationships.

Who we are and how we relate to others are far more valuable than what we have and how much we have achieved. Many couples are both on the treadmill of 40-50 hour work weeks in order to provide things for their children they never had when they were growing up. But are "things" what our children need? Or do they need us and our relationships? ♥

Inside My Open Heart...

My Thoughts & Feelings Today   *Date:*

**"The greatest of achievements
cannot compare with the
greatest relationships."**

My Thoughts & Feelings Today   *Date:*

On Wings Like Eagles

The nature of an eagle causes it to rise **above all the other birds** and living creatures—to get by itself. Eagles are designed to soar. You don't look for an eagle eating in your front yard with the robins and sparrows. The eagle is to all the other birds what the lion is to the animal kingdom. That's why nations have adopted the eagle as a symbol.

The eagle has the ability to rise above all the rest. It is seen as superior—supreme. There is something in the spirit of the eagle that is not easily conquered. They do not make good pets, because they have difficulty being confined to a pen. They want to fly freely—up where the air is clear and the winds are invigorating.

Is that what you would like to do—get some fresh air in your lungs and clean air under your wings? But instead you feel like you are limping along on the ground with most of your soaring strength drained right out of you. Well, there is hope. There is a promise for you.

The Bible says, "... those who hope in the Lord will renew their strength. They will soar on wings like eagles; they will run and not grow weary, they will walk and not be faint" (Isaiah 40:31). That sounds almost too good to be true. But notice that such help only comes when we put our hope in the One who can renew us. ♥

Inside My Open Heart...

My Thoughts & Feelings Today   *Date:*

"There is something in the spirit of the eagle that is not easily conquered."

My Thoughts & Feelings Today   *Date:*

Impact
Of Music

Responding to insistent alarms, the firemen quickly donned their working attire and hurried to their posts. With sirens blaring, the fire trucks sped to the Symphony Hall in Atlanta, Georgia.

Much to the firemen's surprise and relief, it was a false alarm. It seems that the performance of Tchaikovsky's 1812 Overture under the direction of Robert Shaw had set off the delicate alarm system. Music was indeed the hot topic of conversation in Atlanta that night.

Music! It has a great impact on all of us. James Bramston wrote that "Music hath charms to soothe the savage beast." Beethoven said that "music should strike fire from the heart of man and bring tears from the eyes of woman."

Couples court and fall in love while listening to romantic ballads. Moms rock babies to sleep crooning gentle soft lullabies. Music meets many needs and suits different situations.

Music plays an important role in our worship services. We praise the Lord in joyful song for all that He is and will be. Music lifts our hearts and lightens our steps. It soothes us when we're tired and tense.

Music feeds our spirit and nourishes our very soul. It often touches us more effectively than conversation does. The Lord has placed an appreciation of beautiful music within each of us. Let us enjoy this blessing to the fullest!
♥

Inside My Open Heart...

My Thoughts & Feelings Today   *Date:*

"Music lifts our hearts and lightens our steps. It soothes us when we're tired and tense."

My Thoughts & Feelings Today   *Date:*

Through The Valley

In many parts of the world, the sheep are slowly led up the mountain slopes in the Spring and returned to the fold in the Fall. The sheep and the shepherd enjoy the most intimate contact when they are alone in the mountains.

You may have heard someone talking about a mountain top experience. Those are the times when we seem to be able to draw closest to the Lord. We would like to stay on the mountain top all the time, but life isn't that way. When we come down from the mountain, there are valleys to go through.

"Yea though I walk through the valley," the Psalmist said. He had in mind some of the valleys of life—the difficult times that perplex the human spirit. You may be in difficult circumstances right now—circumstances that are sapping your physical and emotional energy. You don't know which way to turn. That's where the Shepherd comes in. The sheep did not fear the valleys, because they knew the shepherd was with them.

Corrie Ten Boom, a lady who spent several years in a German prison camp, once said that she would rather walk with God in the darkness than by herself in the light. We should not be surprised when some of those who seem to be the most peaceful in times of adversity are those who rely upon an intimate fellowship with the Shepherd when walking through the valley. ♥

Inside My Open Heart...

My Thoughts & Feelings Today   *Date:*

"The sheep did not fear the valleys, because they knew the shepherd was with them."

My Thoughts & Feelings Today   *Date:*

Looking Glad, Not Glum

A **little girl from a very poor home was taken to a hospital.** When carolers stopped by her room, it was the first time she had ever heard the Christmas story about why Jesus had come into the world. She accepted Him with the simple faith of a little child. Her heart was filled with joy and a new peace.

The thought of going back to her humble home did not seem to dampen the little girl's spirits. She said to one of the nurses, "I will be taking Jesus with me." The nurse acknowledged that she understood what the girl was talking about.

"Oh, you know Him, too?" the little girl responded.

"Yes," said the nurse.

With a puzzled look on her face, the little girl blurted out, "Well, you don't look like you know Him!"

The nurse was curious, "How do I look?"

"Well, I thought that if you knew Him you wouldn't look so glum. I thought you would look glad," the little girl commented.

After the child left the hospital, the nurse couldn't forget her brief encounter with the little girl who had been touched by the Christmas story. Nor could she forget the simple honesty of the child who had reminded her that when Jesus touches our heart, His presence needs to reach our face. ♥

Inside My Open Heart...

My Thoughts & Feelings Today   *Date:*

"...when Jesus touches our heart, His presence needs to reach our face."

My Thoughts & Feelings Today   *Date:*

Heirlooms

One Christmas, my wife's cousin had his home broken into. All the presents under the tree were stolen—along with a number of cherished hand-me-downs.

Several hunting guns from her grandfather were among the items lost. Although not particularly valuable, they carried with them many memories. They were heirlooms: family keepsakes that Greg would have eventually passed down to his sons.

No doubt your family has some heirlooms—maybe a crystal bowl that has been passed down from one generation to another or a grandfather clock that goes back several generations or a night stand built by your great-grandfather. You value and preserve it, because you long to pass it on to the next generation.

There are other things that we also want to pass on to the next generation, but they are not physical and material. They are the most valuable heirlooms we possess—values, character, morals, and spiritual virtues. They are the stuff of which life is made.

You help preserve these heirlooms for the next generation when you live these values in your own life. As younger family members and friends watch and observe, many will want to be like you. They will hold tightly to the moral and spiritual qualities they learned from you. ♥

Inside My Open Heart...

My Thoughts & Feelings Today   Date:

**"...the most valuable heirlooms
we possess—values, character,
morals, and spiritual virtues."**

My Thoughts & Feelings Today   Date:

It's What's Inside

South African Archbishop Desmond Tutu once told about a little boy who was watching a man selling balloons. Every so often the balloon seller would release a balloon into the air to draw attention to his product. Finally the boy approached the man and said, "Excuse me, sir. How come when you let go of a balloon—a green balloon, white balloon, red balloon, or even a black balloon—they always float up into the sky?"

The man replied, "Son, it's not the color of the balloon that matters. It's the stuff inside."

Oh, how true that is! It does matter greatly what's on the inside.

Our three boys did not get their growth spurts until the latter part of their high school years. Consequently they were smaller than most of the boys against whom they competed in sports. Frequently they heard me remind them, "It's not the size of the dog in the fight, but the size of the fight in the dog." They heard it so often they started quoting it whenever they thought I was about to share the wisdom with them again.

Jesus reminded us that what a man really is flows from his heart, his being inside him (Mark 7:21). It doesn't matter what he looks like, the color of his skin, what side of the tracks he was born on or who his parents are. His inner spirit is what really counts. ♥

Inside My Open Heart...

My Thoughts & Feelings Today   *Date:*

"Jesus reminded us that what a man really is flows from his heart, his being inside him..."

My Thoughts & Feelings Today   *Date:*

In His Shadow

While delivering papers as a young boy and teen, I could easily be engulfed with fear by the many strange sights and sounds along my early morning path. I can remember riding my bike under a dimly lit street light or walking to the side door of one of the houses and being startled by this "thing" near me. All of a sudden, it would jump out in front of me, off to my side, or up in back of me. More than once, it spooked me and kept me looking back over my shoulder.

What was chasing me? Nothing more than my shadow. It taught me an important lesson, even though I didn't particularly appreciate it at the time. I learned that the source of the shadow is never far away.

Psalms 91:1 says that "He who dwells in the shelter of the Most High will rest in the shadow of the Almighty." These are words of assurance and comfort. God is not far away from those who trust in Him. God's shadow provides shade and protection for His weary travelers and pilgrims. Can't you just picture the Lord hovering over them and maintaining a watch—just like parents sitting on the porch looking out for the well being of their children playing in the yard.

Today as you go about your tasks, picture in your mind the shadow of God covering you. Rather than feeling frightened, be strengthened in knowing that you are protected by a mighty God. His shadow falling upon your life is something beautiful and wonderful. Always remember that God is close by, watching over you. ♥

Inside My Open Heart...

My Thoughts & Feelings Today   Date:

"... you are protected by a mighty God... His shadow falling upon your life..."

My Thoughts & Feelings Today   Date:

References

4. *The Autoillustrator* (a computerized illustration program), # 6184, P.O. Box 5056, Greeley, CO 80632, 1993.

6. *500 Clean Jokes and Humorous Stories and How to Tell Them*, Barbour, Westwood, New Jersey, 1985, page 9.

10. *The Autoillustrator*, #6282.

12. Written by Colleen Baron, edited by Bill Hossler. (Biblical quotes are from *The Good News Bible*.)

14. *The Autoillustrator*, #5292, #9016.

16. *The Autoillustrator*, #5924.

20. *Leadership Journal*, Winter 1986, Vol. VII, No. 1, page 41, 465 Gundersen Drive, Carol Stream, IL 60188.

22. *Leadership Journal*, Fall 1985, Vol. VI, No. 4, page 77.

24. *The Computer Assistant* (a computerized illustration program), "A Prejudiced Usher," 6100 Wooded Edge Court, Arlington, TX 76017.

26. *The Autoillustrator*, #6167.

28. *The Autoillustrator*, #6108.

30. *The Autoillustrator*, #6334.

32. *The Autoillustrator*, #10552

34. *The Autoillustrator*, #2947

36. *The Autoillustrator*, #8784

38. *The Autoillustrator*, #11823

40. *The Computer Assistant*, #104

42. Written by Colleen Baron, edited by Bill Hossler.

44. *Leadership Journal*, Spring 1985, Vol. 7, No. 2, page 68.

46. *The Autoillustrator*, #13049.

48. *Leadership Journal*, Winter 1986, Vol. 7, No. 2, page 40.

50. *The Autoillustrator*, #12,499.

52. *The Autoillustrator*, #6287

54. *Leadership Journal*, Fall 1995, Vol. 16, No. 4, p. 40.

58. *Leadership Journal*, Vol. 13, No. 2.

64. *Leadership Journal*, Vol. 13, No. 2.

66. *The Living Bible*, Tyndale House Publishers, Wheaton, IL 1971, p. 655.

68. *The Autoillustrator*, #4962.

70. *The Autoillustrator*, #12648.

72. Written by Colleen Baron, edited by Bill Hossler.

76. *The Autoillustrator*, #11923.

82. *The Autoillustrator* #4159.

86. *The Banner* (weekly newsletter of the Broadmoor Baptist Church, 4110 Youree Dr., Shreveport, LA 71105), October 9, 1995, Vol 54, No. 43.

88. *The Autoillustrator,* #4965.

92. *The Autoillustrator,* #98.

94. Written by Colleen Baron, edited by Bill Hossler.

96. *The Autoillustrator,* #12645.

100. *The Computer Assistant,* #592.

104. *450 Stories from Life,* Judson Press, 1947, pages 214-215.

108. *The Autoillustrator,* #12184.

110. *The Autoillustrator,* #5060, #5061.

112. *The Computer Assistant,* #786.

114. *The Autoillustrator,* #12,940.

116. *The Computer Assistant,* "Go For The Gold."

118. Written by Terry Pettee, edited by Bill Hossler.

120. *The Computer Assistant,* #1999.

124. *The Autoillustrator,* #10164.

126. *The Computer Assistant,* #1238.

128. *28 Unbreakable Laws of Life,* Max Anders

130. *The Autoillustrator,* #4053.

132. *The Autoillustrator,* #4925.

136. *The Autoillustrator,* #7004, #7005, #7006, #8782.

140. *The Autoillustrator,* #4036.

144. *The Computer Assistant,* #1434.

146. *The Autoillustrator,* #4698, #6054.

148. *The Autoillustrator,* #5105.

152. Written by Colleen Baron, edited by Bill Hossler

154. *The Computer Assistant,* #954.

156. Written by Colleen Baron, edited by Bill Hossler

158. *The Computer Assistant,* "How To Manage Stress."

160. *The Computer Assistant,* #136.

162. *The Computer Assistant,* "The Lady or the Tiger."

166. *The Autoillustrator,* #4884.

168. *Leadership Journal, Winter 1995, Vol. 16, #1, page 39.*

170. *The Computer Assistant,* #394, #134.

174. *The Computer Assistant,* Psychotherapy-Marriage."

178. *The Computer Assistant,* #373.

180. *The Autoillustrator,* #3916.

182. *The Autoillustrator,* #4564.

184. *The Autoillustrator,* #5973, 6104.

186. *The Autoillustrator,* #8787, 11917.

190. Written by Colleen Baron edited by Bill Hossler

194. *The Computer Assistant,* #443.

198. *The Computer Assistant,* "It's What's Inside."

Key Publishing Company
Key Publishing is a not-for-profit organization that exists to encourage aspiring new Christian writers to publish good Christian literature that might otherwise remain unavailable. Unsolicited manuscripts are accepted, but authors should request a copy of our style guidelines.

We Welcome Your Thoughts...
We would like to hear how your life has been blessed by Bill Hossler's *Keys To Open Your Heart.*

Contact Us Today!
    Write: Key Publishing
    3240 Pine Grove Avenue
    Port Huron, Michigan 48060
    Or FAX: 1-810-984-5595

Please let us know if we have your permission to use your comments in our promotional materials.

Also Available From Key Publishing Company

Goodbye Darwin
A Handbook for Young Adults
by Art Cooper

Students in select Christian schools
throughout the country now use this guide to
better understand the many flaws in Charles
Darwin's Theory of Evolution. Written in
direct, easy-to-follow language by a
professional scientist with a firm grasp
of the material.

110 pages • 5 1/2 x 8 1/2 • Trade Paper • Youth/
Young Adult Science

KEY PUBLISHING • ISBN 0-9650491-0-8 • $7.95

Radical Promises
For Desperate Times
How God Gets You Through
by Bill Hossler

"Bill Hossler is as practical as Monday morning.
Practical, Simple, Basic, Biblical... easy to apply
TODAY! If you take one tenth of the truth from this
book into your life, you will never be the same."
—Bobb Biehl, President, Masterplanning Group
International

For people looking for answers to tough questions, this book
offers hope, encouragement, and faith-building principles. Those who
know the Lord will be refreshed. Seekers will find direction and practical
insight into the process of Christianity.

152 pages • 6 x 9 • Trade Paper • Devotional

KEY PUBLISHING • ISBN 0-9650491-1-6 • $12.95